INTERNATIONAL BUSINESS ETIQUETTE

Asia & The Pacific Rim

What You Need To Know To Conduct
Business Abroad with Charm and Savvy

By
Ann Marie Sabath

CAREER PRESS
3 Tice Road
P.O. Box 687
Franklin Lakes, NJ 07417
1-800-CAREER-1
201-848-0310 (NJ and outside U.S.)
Fax: 201-848-1727

INTERNATIONAL BUSINESS ETIQUETTE: ASIA & THE PACIFIC RIM

Cover design by Design Solutions
Printed in the U.S.A. by Book-mart Press

To order this title, please call toll-free 1-800-CAREER-1 (NJ and Canada: 201-848-0310) to order using VISA or MasterCard, or for further information on books from Career Press.

Library of Congress Cataloging-in-Publication Data

Sabath, Ann Marie.
    International business etiquette : Asia & the Pacific Rim : what you need to know to conduct business abroad with charm and savvy / by Ann Marie Sabath.
        p. cm.
    Includes index.
    ISBN 1-56414-373-2 (pbk.)
    1. Business etiquette—Asia—Case studies. 2. Business etiquette--Pacific Area—Case studies. 3. National characteristics—Case studies. I. Title.
    HF5389.3.A78S23   1999
    395.5'2'095—dc21   98-42350

Acknowledgments

My acknowledgments go to...

That man of international vision, my publisher, Ron Fry.

My editor, Sue Gruber, who transformed the manuscript into its finished form.

My mother and dear friend, Mary Amelia Abraham Sabath, for our precious time together.

My dad, who is always only one telephone call away.

My children, Scott Jason and Amber Marie Wert, who held down the family fort during the hours I spent writing this book.

Dearest Thomas Byron, who continues to be a sounding board for me.

The librarians and librarian assistants of the Public Library of Cincinnati and Hamilton County for their infinite patience in answering my questions for this book.

My research assistant, Julie Brigner.

My travel companions to Asia, Elaine Green and Nonnie Cameron.

My literary agent, Brandon Toropov, who made this book a reality.

Contents

Introduction

No matter where you go in the world or what you're doing, there is always a "proper" way to do things. Becoming knowledgeable in every country's "silent language" of etiquette is therefore essential for developing good business relationships overseas. This certainly holds true in Asia and the Pacific Rim, but with so much diversity in this area of the world, how do you know what is considered "proper" in each country?

International Business Etiquette: Asia and the Pacific Rim addresses the do's and don'ts of 13 countries, including Australia, China, Hong Kong, Indonesia, Japan, Malaysia, New Zealand, The Philippines, Singapore, South Korea, Taiwan, Thailand, and Vietnam.

The goal of this book is to help you overcome any hesitation you may have about doing the right thing in each situation and to prepare you for doing business abroad so that you will represent your organization, your country, and yourself in the best manner possible. The book is meant to give you just that "polish" you need for increasing your profits in Asia and the Pacific Rim.

Each chapter of the book begins with an overview of the country and some important facts and statistics, followed by points of etiquette, and then several "Whatever you do..." tips. These tips are meant to raise your level of awareness regarding how the customs and manners of the country you will be visiting may be different from the ones you are accustomed to. Some chapters, including this introduction, end with words of advice from actual businesspeople who have successfully conducted business abroad. Their recommendations are great for keeping the sand out of your international social gears.

Each chapter addresses the most pertinent points of etiquette that are essential for becoming familiar with that nation's mores. You will see many similarities among some of the countries, such as how business cards are exchanged, the way a smile should be interpreted, which seat is considered the seat of honor, the importance of maintaining harmony with others or "saving face," what to observe when going into a temple or mosque, and so on. Conversely, you will learn that some countries' customs are as different as night and day, such as whether it is acceptable to burp after a meal, or whether you are allowed to blow your nose or chew gum in public. Knowing these points of etiquette may be crucial to successful relationships overseas.

Several chapters have sections that are culture-specific—for example, advice on business-card etiquette or the proper use of chopsticks. Areas addressed that are common to most countries include:

Statistics and Information

Air Travel

This section will familiarize you with the names of the main airport(s) for each country. It also will give you some tips on how to get from the airport to the heart of the city. Note: In most chapters, the airport(s) described is/are the one(s) closest to that country's capital.

Country Codes

This section will come in handy when you are communicating with overseas clients from your home and also when you are abroad and someone from your office wants to call or fax you. In many of the sections, you will be provided with the country code, the city codes within that nation, and the number(s) not to dial when you are dialing a number within the country you're visiting. Note that in some countries, local telephone numbers consist of seven digits, while in other countries, it may be necessary to dial eight numbers when making a local call.

When making international calls, first dial 011, followed by the country code, then the phone number. When calling collect, 01 should be dialed, followed by the country code and phone number. In some countries, telephones are certain colors based their availability for local, out-of-town, or out-of-country calls.

Currency

This section describes the currency of each country and the various denominations of notes and coins. In addition, you will learn where you can get the best currency exchange rates in each of the 13 countries covered in this book.

Dates

Did you know that in some Asian and Pacific Rim countries, the day is written before the month, while in other countries, the year precedes the month and the day? In one Asian country, the calendar year dates from when the republic was formed. After reading this section, you will recognize the importance of writing out months in letters rather than in numbers, in order to avoid any miscommunication about dates.

Ethnic Makeup

You may find it helpful to know what ethnicities predominate in the country you are visiting. This section summarizes which ethnic groups form the majority of the population, and what other peoples may be encountered in a particular country.

Holidays

This section will give you a listing of the various holidays that are celebrated in each country. By having these dates close at hand, you will be better prepared when you encounter closed offices. You will also know when to schedule meetings and what dates to avoid.

Language

This section describes the official or predominant language spoken in each country. Note that many of the Asian and Pacific Rim countries addressed in this book teach English as a second national language in schools. For that reason, in many countries, you will hear English spoken as frequently as you will hear Chinese if you are in Singapore or Cantonese if you are in China. However, don't allow yourself to be tricked into believing that individuals in these countries have the same Western values and attitudes that you do simply because they are speaking your language.

Religion

In many countries, religion is a way of life for its people. You will find different religious customs as you travel through Asia and the Pacific Rim. In some nations, people practice only Buddhism, while in other countries, the Anglican or Catholic religions are observed. Islam is popular in such locales as Malaysia, the Philippines, and Indonesia. You may even find people who observe as many as three religions in the country you're visiting. Similarly it may seem to you that in some countries there are temples and/or mosques on every other street corner, yet there are other countries, such as Japan, where religious beliefs are less likely to be expressed publicly. It is helpful to know what religions predominate in the country you are visiting. Just remember that in most cases, a person's religious preferences should not be a topic of conversation!

Time Zone Differences

When you are away, you may need or want to stay in touch with both family and the office. The information in this section will assist you in knowing the time of day it is back home, so that you don't awaken a family member out of a deep sleep or get only voice mail when you need to call your assistant back at the office.

Weather

Depending on where you are from and the Asian or Pacific Rim country you will be visiting, you may experience higher temperatures and humidity than you may have ever encountered in your life. According to the time of the year you will be traveling, you may even experience some very cold weather. This section is meant to familiarize you with the kind of temperatures you will encounter.

Etiquette

Business Attire

This section will assist you in projecting the appropriate image based on what is considered acceptable business dress in a particular country. You will find that in some countries, it is so hot and humid that short-sleeved shirts, ties, and tailored trousers are considered proper professional attire, whereas in other countries, a jacket is in order with those short-sleeved shirts. In still other Asian and Pacific Rim countries, appropriate business attire will consist of a suit with a long-sleeved shirt, or sport coat and trousers. For women, it is often better to pack more skirts than slacks, and to wear tops with sleeves rather than the sleeveless variety. When choosing skirts, be sure to select ones that are of a conservative length.

Knowing in advance what is customary or acceptable in a particular country will help you accordingly in packing clothes for your business trip. This section shows you how.

Business Entertaining/Dining

In many Asian and Pacific Rim countries, entertaining and dining are vital to establishing business relationships. Therefore, good table manners are essential, and you need to know if there are any customs that you can and should observe when dining in a non-Western country. This section helps to save you from embarrassment by addressing the do's and don'ts when hosting meals and being hosted, as well as the ins and outs of dining in restaurants. It covers many of the finer points of etiquette, such as when you should or should not replenish your own beverage, when you will be offered chopsticks or a spoon and fork, what food you may be offered, when it is considered good form to leave food on your plate, and much more. Finally, this section will emphasize the importance of referring to the check as the "bill" in Asian and Pacific Rim countries.

Conversation

Part of establishing rapport is knowing what to talk about with whom and when. Knowing what topics of conversation are appropriate should certainly be common sense; some may relate to the culture and customs of the country you are visiting. In certain countries, you will find that it may be better not to mention other Asian countries. Because many ethnic groups are superstitious, you also may find certain topics off limits.

This section will not only suggest topics to approach or avoid, it will also help to prepare you for the questions you may be asked, especially if they are questions that you would consider too personal. By preparing yourself in this way, you won't look shocked when you hear such questions coming at you. You also will know how to answer them in a vague manner that allows the person asking them to save face.

Gestures and Public Manners

This is one of the most important sections in this book, as it will help you mind your "nonverbal manners." You will learn when eye contact and physical touch (even a handshake) may be considered offensive, as well as when a smile is more than just a smile. You will also learn the do's and don'ts of riding on public transportation, chewing gum in public, and using the proper hand when offering or receiving something.

Actions that you take for granted can be very offensive in many Asian and Pacific Rim countries. For that reason, helpful advice on gestures has also been incorporated into this section. This includes knowing, among other things, the appropriate way to beckon another person, where spitting is acceptable and in which countries it is considered an offense, how to show respect when you are passing two people, how to point to another person or an object (in some cases done by puckering your lips!), how to say "no" using a hand gesture, where to rub or scratch to show you are ashamed or embarrassed, and so on.

Gift-giving Etiquette

In most of the Asian and Pacific Rim countries, gift-giving is an important part of developing a professional (or personal) relationship. For that reason, this section has been included so that you know which countries you should visit with a gift in hand. You also will learn what to take and the numbers to avoid when giving multiple gifts. Finally, because colors signify many things to Asians, you also will learn what colors to use or avoid for gift-wrap, and how to wrap.

Greetings and Introductions

When do you bow and how low should you go? Should you be the first to initiate a handshake? If so, with whom should you shake first? When should you wait to extend your hand and what about shaking hands with women? What about the business-card exchange? At what part of a greeting should this "ceremony" take place? These and many other answers to greetings and introductions are addressed in this section. In some countries, the business-card exchange is of such importance that it has been given a section of its own.

Meeting Manners

If you will be conducting business in an Asian or Pacific Rim country, this will be a very important section for you. You will learn in which countries to make small talk before starting a meeting and in which countries it is better to keep chatter to a minimum and get down to business. You will also learn such particulars as when phrases such as "I understand" or "we will see" will actually mean "no." Other points covered include understanding the importance of age and rank, as well as the negotiating and decision-making process. Note: For a few of the countries covered, there will be a related section on "How Decisions Are Made."

Punctuality

Isn't it funny how we all have the same amount of time each day and yet people use (or abuse) it so differently? You will find that individuals from some Asian and Pacific Rim countries are very relaxed about time commitments, while others place great importance on punctuality. In some cases, while you may be kept waiting, you will not be looked upon in a favorable manner if you keep others waiting. You will therefore learn where your tardiness may be overlooked and where being late may get you off on the wrong foot and perhaps even sever ties. This section will also reveal which countries' deadlines are not viewed with the same finality as they may be in the West.

Seating Etiquette

Unlike the Western culture, in most Asian and Pacific Rim countries, there is a seat of honor that is designated for the most important guest or the highest-ranking person at a meeting—and sometimes that person is you! Thus, whether you will be in a meeting or at a formal meal, this section will help you understand which seat to offer your guest of honor and where you should be seated in relation to that person.

Tipping Tips

This section will cover who you should tip and when, as well as when it is considered an insult to tip and when you should simply leave a handful of change as gratuity.

When You Are Invited to Another Person's Home

In some countries, it is rare to be invited to a home. When you are, that person may consider it an honor to share his or her personal life with you. In many chapters, this section addresses when to arrive, what to have in hand, if your shoes should be removed, the role of the host's spouse, and how you will know it is time to depart. You also will learn in which country it is a major faux pas to refer to your host's spouse as a "hostess."

Women in Business

This section explains how Western businesswomen fare in certain countries. You will find that in some Asian and Pacific Rim countries, it will come as a surprise that a Western woman is a key player in the decision-making process, while in others, it is considered quite common and acceptable. This section also reveals who should initiate a handshake, the importance of conservative clothing, and taboos concerning women.

Advice From the Experts

"Mean what you say and do what you mean. Trust is hard enough to earn and even harder over the great pond—the Pacific."

—*John Balanda, President, Pacific Corporation*

"Never write on a business card. It is a sign of disrespect."

—*Pat Cronenberg, CEO, Pier 'N Port Travel*

"Most Asian business cards have an English side and a native side. If the English side does not have an 'English name' or translation, make sure you check the pronunciation of the person's name. Also, if you have a name that is difficult to pronounce, suggest an alternative. For instance, I usually introduce myself as 'Doug,' but most Asians pronounce it as 'duck' or 'dog,' which they know is incorrect. I have found through experience that 'Douglas' is easier for them to use. So in Asia, I am 'Douglas.'"

—*Douglas E. Darrow, International Operations Quality Leader, General Electric Aircraft Engine Services*

"[Regarding women]...I have found that the lack of respect is a huge problem throughout Asia. American businessmen should not follow the lead of Asian businessmen in both corporate and social interactions with women. Common courtesy and respect should dictate your every move. That may mean politely refusing prostitution in Thailand and Indonesia...."

—*Gregory Caraboolad, Chief Tooling Engineer for PMC Industries, a machine tool builder serving the gas and oil industry*

Chapter 1

Australia

10 reasons people do business in Australia

1. Australia is situated in the fastest-growing region internationally.

2. Its location makes it simple to do business with other Asian countries.

3. The Australian government encourages international growth.

4. The government has modified its regulations to encourage free trade.

5. As an English-speaking country, there are few language barriers.

6. Australians typically do not engage in long "courtships" before making business decisions.

7. Historically, this country is known for its agricultural strengths, especially wheat, cotton, fruit, and sugar. It is also rich in minerals such as bauxite, coal, copper, iron, lead, tin, uranium, and zinc.

8. It is known for its strength in manufacturing and service areas.

9. This country is a world leader in research and development, along with technological innovation.

10. Australia's tourism is on the increase.

Australia—also known as "The Land Down Under"—is located in the south Pacific Ocean, southeast of Indonesia and west of New Zealand. It is the only country in the world that is also a continent. Its capital is Canberra. Originally occupied by natives called Aborigines, the land was colonized by the British beginning in the late 1700s. For a time, Australia was a penal colony—many of the early settlers were prisoners sent there to carry out their jail terms in hard labor on the arid continent. Today Australia, whose people are often affectionately referred to as "Aussies," is a thriving Western democracy, with a system of government that is based mostly on the British parliamentary system and partly on the U.S. system of interdependent national and state governments.

Australia uses a decimal currency of dollars and cents. Economically, the country relies heavily on trade with the rest of the world, especially the Asia region, where more than 60 percent of its exports are sent. In addition to a variety of other goods, Australia is the world's largest exporter of meat.

As the world's sixth-largest country, Australia boasts a population of more than 18.3 million people, more than 85 percent of whom live in cities along the coasts. The country is divided into six states and two territories: Queensland, New South Wales, South Australia, Tasmania, Victoria, Western Australia, the Northern Territory, and the Australian Capital Territory. While mostly a dry continent, it also boasts splendid beaches and rain forests, making the country a magnet for tourists who wish to see such attractions as the large outback, and the Great Barrier Reef in Queensland, and animals such as the koala and the kangaroo, which are indigenous only to Australia. In the year 2000, the country will host the Olympic Games in the city of Sydney.

Statistics and Information

Air Travel

Sydney has the most popular international airport for visitors from the North. The Kingsford Smith Airport has two international terminals, one for arrivals and one for departures. When traveling to Sydney from the airport, you have three main transportation options for making the 40-minute trip into the heart of the city. The state-run Airport Express Bus (yellow and green buses) costs adults about A$5. Independent commercial "minibuses" also make the trip for approximately A$5, and taxis will range from A$20 to A$25.

You may also fly into Melbourne's Tullamarine International Airport or Brisbane's Eagle Farm, which opened a new international terminal just a few years ago. For the 12-mile ride into Melbourne, take the Skybus Shuttle Service. It leaves the airport every half-hour and will cost you about A$9. Your best bet into Brisbane is the airport bus. It should take about 20 minutes to reach the city, with the ride costing approximately A$6.50.

Country Code

The country code for Australia is 61.

Australia's city codes are:

• 06 for Canberra.

• 03 for Melbourne.

• 02 for Sydney.

Currency

Australian currency is referred to as bills or notes, and like U.S. currency, it is based on a system of one dollar = 100 cents. Australian and U.S. dollars are differentiated by placing either "A" or "US" before the dollar sign. (For example, $100 in Australian currency is written A$100, while in U.S. currency it is US$100.)

Australian bills or notes come in denominations of A$5, A$10, A$20, A$50, and A$100. Silver coins break the currency down into 5 cents, 10 cents, 20 cents, 50 cents, and $1. Gold coins of A$1 and A$2 denominations are also common.

Be sure to go to a bank when exchanging money, because you will get the best exchange rate there. Although it may be more convenient to exchange your currency at hotels, you will pay a higher rate for doing so.

When exchanging traveler's checks for Australian currency, be sure to have your passport—you will need it for identification.

Dates

Dates are written differently in Australia than they are in many other countries. The day is placed before the month, followed by the year. For example, January 30, 1999, would be written 30 January 1999, or 30/1/99.

Ethnic Makeup

Australia is made up primarily of Caucasians, approximately 95 percent of whom are of European descent. Individuals of Asian background make up about four percent of the population, while Aborigines and other minorities account for just over 1 percent of the country's ethnic makeup.

Holidays

The following are the days that are considered national celebrations. Most businesses honor these days by being closed, so it is best to avoid scheduling meetings during these times.

177760

January 1	New Year's Day
January 26	Australia Day (a celebration of the first settlement of Australia)
March	Labour Day (first or second Monday of the month)
April	Easter Holiday (celebrated from Good Friday through the following Monday or Tuesday)
April 25	Anzac Day (the national memorial day)
June	Queen's Birthday (second Monday)
August 1 or September 1	Wattle Day*
November	Melbourne's Cup Day (first Tuesday)
November 11	Remembrance Day (commemorates the end of World War II)
December 25	Christmas Day
December 26	Boxing Day (not observed in South Australia)

* The Wattle is a large acacia tree. It is also the national floral emblem of Australia. This day is celebrated in many but not all localities.

Language

Although never made legal, Australia's official language is considered to be English. However, Aussies speak a type of English called "Strine." Many English-speaking people make the assumption that they will have no problem understanding the Australian dialect, but they soon learn they can't always comprehend and assimilate the hybrid version of English that Australians have developed over the years. In fact, words and terms that are frequently used in the United States may have totally different definitions to the Aussies.

Religion

Because Australia was settled mostly by the British, the Anglican and Roman Catholic faiths each account for one quarter of Australian religious preferences. Another quarter is comprised of all other Christian religions, while the rest is divided among a variety of religions, atheism, or agnosticism.

Time Zone Differences

Australia has three time zones:

- *Western Australian Time*, which is 8 hours ahead of Greenwich Mean Time and 13 hours ahead of U.S. Eastern Standard Time. Cities in this time zone include Perth, Fremantle, and Alice Springs.

- *Central Australian Time*, which is 9½ hours ahead of Greenwich Mean Time and 14½ hours ahead of U.S. Eastern Standard Time. Cities in this time zone include Darwin and Adelaide.

- *Eastern Australian Time*, which is 10 hours ahead of Greenwich Mean Time and 15 hours ahead of U.S. Eastern Standard Time. Cities in this time zone include Victoria, Queensland, New South Wales, Tasmania, Brisbane, Sydney, Canberra, Melbourne, and Hobart.

Australian Daylight Savings Time begins on the last Sunday of October and lasts through the last Sunday in March.

Weather

Seasons in Australia are the opposite of those in the northern hemisphere, with winter beginning in June and summer in December. The weather varies greatly depending on location. Most of the country is flat and arid, however the east coast can get as much as 200 inches of rain a year. The northern part of the country gets a lot of tropical weather, while the southeast part, which is where the majority of the population lives, experiences mostly moderate weather (although temperatures over 100 degrees Fahrenheit are commonplace).

Etiquette

Business Attire

Australian business attire for men consists of dark suits and ties, rather than sport coats and trousers. Depending on the weather and also the circumstances, you may also see men in short-sleeved shirts with shorts, a tie, and knee-high socks. Appropriate business dress for women would be suits or professional dresses (no slacks). However, business dress may be less formal in tropical climates than in cities such as Brisbane.

Business Entertaining/Dining

Australian cuisine and dining have been shaped by the English culture, and Americans will be able to find their familiar favorites on all menus. However, there are some distinctly Australian dishes that may appear in front of you. Of course, kangaroo is a favorite, as is the unofficial national dish, the meat pie.

"Bar-b-ques" or barbies are a very popular form of entertainment that takes place in homes. If you are invited to a barbie, be sure to dress casually and get ready for an evening of mixing and mingling.

If someone extends an invitation to you to "tea," recognize that you are being invited to dinner. On the other hand, if someone asks you what you had for "supper" the evening before, the person is referring to the late-night snack that you may have had.

The table setting in Australia will look familiar, as will the dining habits of the Australians around you. However, Aussies are a bit more informal. Eating with your hands is acceptable, as is a more than hearty appetite.

When you are eating and find that you are content, be sure to avoid using the term, "I'm stuffed." This term has a crude connotation in Australia.

When hosting a dinner at a restaurant, you should bring your own alcoholic beverage with you (beer is most common). Most restaurants are not licensed to serve alcohol, and because drinking is a cherished and prided custom, your Australian guest would not look favorably on a meal where beer is not offered.

When you are invited out, whoever extends the invitation pays for the meal.

Conversation

There are very few Australians who ever lack for something to say. In fact, most people who meet them describe Aussies as a very friendly and articulate group.

Few things are deemed to be inappropriate topics of conversation in Australia. If you bring up one such topic, though, don't be surprised if you are told flatly to "mind your own business." You will find Aussies to be very direct.

Aussies love a good debate and are quick-witted conversationalists. Religion and politics are great subjects for discussion. Be prepared for a good battle of words, probably just a test by the Australian you're talking to, to see if you can stand your ground.

Although most topics are fair game, just as in other countries, the subject of race relations is better not discussed.

Don't boast about yourself or your company's accomplishments. Australians value the achievements of a group or community over the individual. They prefer to see achievement in action and make their own decisions about your worth, rather than have you tell them how great you are.

Gestures and Public Manners

It is considered unacceptable for men to touch, pat, or hug other men. The handshake is the most appropriate form of physical contact. Take note that a man will rarely offer his hand to a woman and a woman who takes such initiative will make a man uncomfortable and may even receive a weak response.

When speaking to an Aussie, be sure to maintain an arm's length distance from the person. This will ensure that you are respecting that individual's personal space.

Chivalry and common courtesy, with little thought to class or position, still have a great place in this mellow culture. It is common for men to open doors for women, as well as employees for bosses and youth for elders. It is also common for strangers to greet one another and strike up lively conversations.

When pointing to someone, be sure to do it with your entire hand. Pointing at someone with just your index finger is considered to be offensive.

If it appears that things are going "okay," be sure to verbalize it rather than demonstrating it by placing your thumbs up. Just as with pointing with your index finger, this gesture is considered rude.

While a wink may be a harmless nonverbal form of communication, men should nonetheless avoid winking at women.

If you have an allergy or cold, be sure to blow your nose in private. Doing so in public is considered offensive.

Gift-giving Etiquette

Although gift-giving is not as common in Australia as it is in other countries, it is appropriate to go with something in hand if you are invited to the home of an Aussie. Recommended items include something commemorative of the country or city you represent or a box of quality chocolates. The most important rule to remember when exchanging gifts with Australians is that your thoughtfulness matters more than the cost of the gift.

Greetings and Introductions

Everyone is familiar with the indigenous "G'day, mate" heard in almost every television program and film about Australia. This is actually accurate. Regardless of how well people know each other, this is the common casual greeting—especially between individuals who have already established a rapport.

Fitting in with the laid-back demeanor in which business and life in general is conducted in Australia, titles are not commonplace, and in fact, are frowned upon as pretentious and showy. For that reason, do not flaunt your title. Although it may be important for introductions in some cultures, this is not the case in Australia. If you verbalize your title when meeting an Aussie, you may be perceived as bragging.

Even recent acquaintances address one another, both in person and in correspondence, by their first names. However, it is in order to wait for an Aussie to invite you to do this. Until that invitation is extended, last names preceded by Mr., Mrs., or Ms. should be used.

How Decisions Are Made

Most decisions are made by management and those with authority, with the good of the whole in mind. There is much more collaboration among co-workers than is found in wholly autocratic work environments. Subordinates are consulted and their opinions are given much weight. For that reason alone, be prepared for decision-making to be a lengthy process. Whatever you do, do not rush an Australian if you are interested in developing a long-term relationship with that person.

Meeting Manners

Get to the point. Although small talk is part of the relationship-building process in many cultures, one important tip to keep in mind while conducting business with Australians is that words are taken at face value. For that reason, be direct. Say what you have to say and expect your words to be taken literally. In return, you will be expected to interpret what Aussies say to you in the same direct manner.

When discussing business, be especially accurate and to the point. Because work is perceived by Aussies to be a necessary evil, recognize that the use of elaborate speech is laborious to Australians who would probably prefer to be discussing topics other than business.

Punctuality

Although being on time is a good business practice to be followed around the globe, it is important to recognize that Aussies are very relaxed about time. Therefore, if you are a few minutes late for a meeting, it will be overlooked. In turn, if you are kept waiting for a few minutes, understand that this is considered acceptable.

Taxi Etiquette

Although it is in order for men to sit in the front with the driver, this is not the case for women. A woman traveling alone should sit in the back left passenger seat of the car (the driver will be on the right).

Tipping Tips

Tipping is rarely necessary and is sometimes considered offensive. One reason is that Australians do not emphasize the differences between social classes. Therefore, if you tip, you may be perceived as implying that you view yourself as "above" that person socially. This rule applies to cab drivers, sky caps, hotel staff, and restaurant servers. However, although service people do not expect to be tipped by the "locals," it is understood that Westerners are accustomed to giving tips in the United States and other countries. Thus, tourists in Australia may offer tips if they so choose and will find their tips to be accepted gratefully.

When You Are Invited to an Australian Home

Be prepared to be treated like one of the family. Rather than being served food and drink, you will most likely be told where things are and to "help yourself." Don't be shy. Dig right in to show you are comfortable and enjoying your visit.

It is customary for guests to take beer or a bottle of wine to their host.

Whatever You Do...

- Don't sit in the back seat of a cab if you are a man.
- Don't make a lot of small talk before getting down to business.
- Don't expect men to necessarily treat women as equals.
- Don't break eye contact with an Aussie when the person is talking to you.
- Don't address an Aussie by his or her first name until you are invited to do so.

- Don't think you are being invited to get together in the afternoon if you are invited to "tea" with an Aussie. The term "tea" refers to the evening meal.

- Don't blow your nose in public. It is considered rude.

- Don't flaunt your title or brag about yourself.

- Don't rush an Aussie in any way.

- Don't expect to see a lot of formality. Aussies prefer a relaxed atmosphere and aren't concerned with pomp and circumstance.

Chapter 2

China

---

10 reasons people do business in China

1. The Chinese government provides incentives for businesses that are export-oriented.

2. Labor is very low cost (sometimes production is also low).

3. China is a top producer of grain and other crops, including silk, cotton, tea, sugar cane, and tobacco.

4. China is wealthy in mineral and energy resources.

5. It is the world's largest coal producer.

6. Machine building and armaments are an important part of China's economy.

7. Major industries are textiles and apparel.

8. The Chinese welcome and encourage new challenges.

9. The Chinese have infinite patience and stamina—qualities that are necessary to establish business relationships in their country.

10. It takes a lot of banquets and entertaining before any business transaction takes place.

The People's Republic of China, located in eastern Asia, is the third largest country in the world, occupying one-fifteenth of the earth's land mass. Bordered by Russia and Mongolia on the north and the Pacific Ocean on the east, China is comprised of 22 provinces and also includes more than 6,500 islands, with the largest grouping located in the South China Sea. The country's population is more than 1.2 billion inhabitants, of which 30 percent live in the cities and 70 percent live in rural areas. They are comprised of 56 separate nationalities, with the Han clan forming the vast majority, and the remainder being taken up by 55 other ethnic minorities.

China's capital is Beijing. Other cities of importance include Shanghai, Tianjin, and Guangzhou (Canton). China is one of the oldest civilizations in the world, with a written history that goes back more than 4,000 years. The country has a rich and diversified culture, and is also known for its great historical achievements, which include such engineering feats as The Great Wall of China, the Grand Canal, and the Karez irrigation system, as well as being the birthplace of paper-making and printing, gunpowder, and the compass.

In 1949, the Communists rose to power under the leadership of Mao Zedong and have ruled China ever since. According to the law, all nationalities are equal and take part in government administration. The National People's Congress runs the country, with all nationalities equally represented in the Congress and fully protected by the government.

Statistics and Information

Air Travel

The two busiest airports in China for international flights are Beijing Capital International Airport and Shanghai's Hongqiao International Airport.

Beijing Airport has been outgrown by the large number of travelers that go through it on a daily basis, so be sure to arrive early and expect lengthy lines. It is located about 30 minutes from the city, and is best reached by a hotel shuttle. If you choose a taxi, accept a ride only from a cab in an official taxi line since others may be corrupt.

Shanghai's Hongqiao Airport is located 30 minutes from the city. Just as in Beijing, a cab from an official taxi line is the best method for reaching the city.

Country Code

The country code for China is 86.

When you're in China and would like to call someone in one of the following regions, dial the seven-digit number preceded by:

- 01 for Beijing.
- 020 for Guangzhou (Canton).
- 021 for Shanghai.

When you are in a country other than China and would like to call one of these regions, simply dial the area codes without the first 0.

Currency

The currency in China is the *reminbi* (RMB), which means "the people's money." The unit of currency of the RMB is called the *yuan* (the term *kuai* is also used interchangeably). As of this printing, approximately 8.3 *yuan* equal 1 U.S. dollar. Each *yuan* is made up of 100 *fen*.

When exchanging money, be sure to visit The Bank of China, where you will be offered the best rate. Note that you will pay a higher rate when exchanging currency in a hotel. Whatever you do, avoid exchanging currency with individuals you may encounter on the street.

When exchanging traveler's checks for this country's currency, be sure to have your passport—you will need it for identification.

Dates

To avoid confusion, write out the month of the year in letters. If you do write a date in numbers, list the day of the month first, followed by the month, then the year. For example, May 10, 1999, is written 10/5/99.

Ethnic Makeup

More than 90 percent of China is comprised of the Han Chinese. The rest of the population is a blend of many minority types, including Mongolian, Hui, Tibetan, Uygur, and Miao.

Holidays

The following are the holidays that are celebrated throughout the country. It is wise to avoid scheduling meetings during these times.

January 1	New Year's Day
Late January/ February	Spring Festival & Chinese New Year (3 days; the dates vary, depending on the lunar calendar)
March 8	International Working Woman's Day
May 1	Labor Day
May 4	Youth Day
June 1	Children's Day
July 1	Anniversary of the Founding of the Communist Party of China
August 1	People's Liberation Army Day
October 1-2	National Day

Language

Mandarin (also known as *putonghua*, or the common language) is the national language in China. Although this is the most commonly spoken language in the mainland, other dialects of the 55 minority nationalities are heard throughout China. For instance, Cantonese is heard more frequently in southern China and also in Hong Kong.

Putonghua is the common language that the government has been supporting for the last several decades. This Mandarin dialect is actually taught in Chinese schools.

Mandarin is one of the official working languages at the United Nations.

Religion

Most Chinese observe Buddhism, Taoism, and Confucianism. A large percentage also consists of followers of Islam, Catholicism, and Protestantism. It is very common for individuals to practice each of these religions.

Time Zone Differences

China is:

- Eight hours ahead of Greenwich Mean Time.
- 13 hours ahead of U.S. Eastern Standard Time.
- Two hours behind Eastern Australian Time.

Weather

Depending on where you will be, China's climate will vary. For instance, Beijing and Shanghai experience very cold winters and very warm summers. If you are going to be in Southern China during its short winter, prepare for rain by taking an umbrella. If you will be in Guangzhou (Canton), prepare for subtropical weather.

China can be greatly affected by monsoons during March and April, as well as September and October. Prepare to encounter a lot of rain if you are traveling there during these months.

Etiquette

Business Attire

Business professional attire should be worn when interacting with the Chinese. That includes a shirt, tie, trousers, and jacket for men; and for women, a suit consisting of a jacket, blouse, and skirt, or a business dress. What Westerners consider business casual attire should not be worn, because this type of dress is not common at Chinese business gatherings.

Business-card Etiquette

Before going to China, take a look at the way your business card (also called the name card or *ming pian*) is laid out. If your company is prestigious in some way—for example, it is the oldest or largest in your country—be sure this is stated on your business card. Titles help the Chinese determine your decision-making authority, so it is also important to emphasize your title on the card, especially if you are in a senior position.

Be sure to take plenty of business cards, because they will be exchanged with virtually everyone you meet.

One of the first things that you should do when arriving in China is to make arrangements with the hotel concierge to have your business cards translated into Chinese on the reverse side. As in other Asian countries, your card should be presented with both hands, in such a way that the person receiving it doesn't have to turn it to read it.

When receiving another person's name card, take it with both hands and study it for a few seconds before commenting on it. It should then either be laid on the table where you are seated or carefully placed in your business card case if you are standing.

Business Entertaining/Dining

Dining is very much a part of establishing business relationships in China. Entertaining is more common as a lunch or dinner activity, rather than breakfast.

There is a seating etiquette in China, so it is best to wait for the person who has invited you to gesture where you should sit, rather than taking a seat yourself.

It's considered good manners for the host to invite you to begin each course. Until that time, your food and beverage should be left untouched.

Be sure to follow appropriate chopstick etiquette. (See Chopstick Etiquette in Chapter 3.) Your host will probably serve you with the longer chopsticks that have been placed on the table for this purpose. He or she may also use the opposite side of his or her own personal chopsticks to serve you.

During Chinese meals, you may be served one dish for every person at the table. These dishes will be placed on a revolving tray in the center of the table. It is considered good manners to eat a little of everything, even if you don't care for it. Chinese etiquette also dictates that you leave something on your plate during each course to show that you are content with that food.

The Chinese have a ritual called *yum cha*, which means "drinking tea." This beverage is enjoyed in both China and Hong Kong for social purposes. It is used to establish rapport prior to a meeting or during meals, and also to assist digestion after meals. If you have been served a food that requires you to use your hands rather than chopsticks (meat on a bone, for example), you may be served tea to be used for dipping your fingers. Some Westerners mistakenly think this second cup of tea is for drinking. When in doubt, just do what your hosts do. (See also Tea Etiquette in the Hong Kong chapter.)

Slurping soup and belching are considered good manners during meals. These noises are expressions of how much you are enjoying the food.

At the end of a meal, toothpicks will be offered to you. You may use them to remove any food lodged between your teeth. You should do this by covering your mouth with your other hand to conceal the toothpick in your mouth. Toothpicks may also be used between courses. Some people believe that it is a good way to remove the taste of the previous course in preparation for the food that is about to be served.

If you are hosting the meal and it is nearing an end, be sure to ask for the bill (rather than the check).

You will know that the meal is nearing an end when fruit is offered and/or hot towels are served. Shortly after these items are offered, guests should prepare to leave. Note that a host will not initiate the end to a gathering until guests have prepared to depart.

(See also Toasting Etiquette.)

Conversation

Small talk is considered to be important prior to the start of a meeting; therefore, it is helpful to know topics that are considered appropriate. They include the weather, what you've enjoyed about your visit to China, your other travel experiences, and so on.

Questions that Westerners consider forward and even inappropriate are considered acceptable by the Chinese. Such questions may include your salary, your marital status, and the number of children you have. If you prefer not to disclose such information, be indirect with your response. Be sure not to openly shun the questioner. This will spare him or her, and also those around you, from losing face.

Gestures and Public Manners

As in many other Asian countries, it is considered inappropriate to touch another person in public—and that even includes patting the person on the shoulder. However, it is considered acceptable to stand closer than two arm's lengths apart from your Chinese counterpart.

When you would like another person to come near you, the proper way to beckon or get that person's attention is to hold one hand facing down and move your fingers towards you as though you are scratching the palm of your hand.

When you are pointing out something, do so with your entire hand rather than by extending your index finger.

While proper form is very important to the Chinese, it is not the case when standing in line in public settings. For example, if you are trying to catch public transportation, get ready to be pushed and shoved.

While spitting is considered an offense in Singapore, this is not the case in China. In fact, spitting, along with blowing your nose with a hanky, is both common and acceptable.

Gift-giving Etiquette

While it is not necessary to present gifts during your first few meetings, it is a good idea to go prepared with items that are representative of your city or country, such as good quality pens or a paperweight with your organization's logo on it.

As in many other Asian countries, avoid giving clocks, watches, handkerchiefs, and white flowers as gifts, because these items are equated with death. Also stay away from scissors, knives, and other forms of cutlery, which are thought of as severing ties.

It is very important that gifts not be so expensive that you embarrass or oblige your Chinese host to respond in kind.

By going to a meeting with a gift in your briefcase, you will be prepared to reciprocate when you are presented with one. Gifts also will come in handy if someone has done a special favor for you.

The recommended color of wrapping paper is red.

When you present a gift to your Chinese client, recognize that it may be refused the first few times out of politeness. You also should go through the ritual of refusing a gift a few times before accepting it.

Once a gift is accepted, it should be opened in private rather than in front of the gift-giver.

If you are presented with eight of something, know that it may not have been by chance. Eight is considered the luckiest of numbers by the Chinese.

Greetings and Introductions

While a bow (from the shoulders) or nod is the typical way for the Chinese to greet each other, the handshake is commonly extended to Westerners as a greeting.

It is important to note that concealing emotion is a part of the Chinese culture. Therefore, don't be surprised if people don't smile as much as you are used to seeing in other countries.

When addressing Chinese individuals, be sure to acknowledge the most senior person first.

Recognize that family names will be the first names you hear, while given names will be the second. Formality is key, so when addressing individuals, the person's family name should be used, followed by his or her first name. For example, "Mr. Chan" would be "Chan Xiansheng." However, when a person has a title, it should precede the given name rather than using "Mr.," "Mrs.," or "Miss." For example, a person with the title of president would be introduced and addressed as "President Chan."

Meeting Manners

The best advice for successfully getting through a Chinese business meeting is to "go with the flow." The Chinese business culture may appear regimented, dictatorial, and rather slow-moving to Westerners. Be sure to allow your Chinese hosts to set the tone by allowing them to initiate greetings, seating suggestions, and negotiations.

The Chinese have a strict hierarchical system and place emphasis on rank. Thus, it would be wise to select one person, usually a senior team member, to be your spokesperson for the group. The Chinese will do the same, and they may become irritated if others attempt to speak out. Although Westerners share power in a discussion setting, in China you should refrain from allowing subordinates to play a role in the proceedings.

Be aware that certain phrases may mean "no." They include "it is inconvenient," "I am not sure," and "maybe."

Punctuality

It is especially important to respect the time a meeting or function is scheduled to begin. In fact, whether you are hosting or attending a function, it is even appropriate to arrive a quarter of an hour earlier than the appointed time, because your Chinese counterpart may also arrive early.

Seating Etiquette

When you are the guest of honor for any occasion, business or personal, expect to be offered the seat in the middle of the table, facing the door. Your host will sit directly across from you. All others should be seated in descending order, based on hierarchy. When you are hosting a meal, be sure to offer the center seat to your most senior guest.

Tipping Tips

While tipping is not expected from other locals, it is expected by individuals traveling to China. In many situations, rather than leaving a percentage of the bill, it is considered acceptable to leave a handful of change (for cab drivers and servers, for example).

Toasting Etiquette

While many countries serve wine as the main alcoholic beverage during formal dinners and banquets, this is not the case in China, where beer is the most common drink. You will usually find three glasses on the table. The largest one should be used for your first choice of beverage (beer, bottled water, or soda). The mid-sized glass will be a wine glass and the smallest one will be for shots of *mgotai*, or sorghum liquor.

If you are a guest, it will be considered appropriate for your host to propose a toast either after the first of several courses has arrived or at the end of the first course. Toasts also will be proposed throughout the meal. Two common toasts are *ganbei* ("bottoms up") and *kai pay* ("empty your glass").

When You Are Invited to a Chinese Home

The Chinese enjoy having visitors in their homes and often center an invitation around a meal. Arrive on time, not too early. Prepare to be asked to remove your shoes.

Chinese homes will be beautifully decorated with mirrors, statues, and the like. Many of these "knickknacks" have significant religious meaning, so it is best to look at them without touching.

Wait until you are invited by your host before sitting down. The guest of honor customarily sits to the left of the host.

Women in Business

Although conditions have greatly improved during recent years, women are still on the climb towards equality in China. In fact, the government has made gender equality one of its goals. There are many Chinese women working, yet few hold leadership positions.

Women should realize that they may have to work harder to be accepted by their Chinese associates; however, it will happen. Western women visiting China should not expect any special attention just because they are women.

Whatever You Do...

- Don't be surprised if you are applauded when first meeting your Chinese contacts. This nonverbal display is a common part of a Chinese greeting and should be reciprocated.

- Don't interpret a "we'll see" as an affirmative answer.

- Don't serve your Chinese host or guest cheese. This food is not common in China, so it may not be compatible with their diet.

- Don't act as though you belong to the "Clean Plate Club." Instead, always leave something on your plate to show that you have been satisfied with that course.

- Don't use red ink when writing. In the eyes of the Chinese, this color of ink implies that you are severing ties.

- Don't be surprised if you are asked questions such as, "How old are you?" or "What is your salary?"

- Don't forget to take gifts. After the first few meetings, you should go with them in hand.

- Don't give gifts in multiples of four. The Cantonese term for "four" is thought to have an unlucky meaning, because it sounds similar to the term for "death."

- Don't be taken aback if a Chinese person asks you, "Have you eaten?" You are not being asked if you are hungry. It is instead the Chinese way of saying, "How are you?"

- Don't believe that you are being complimented if you are called *yang guai* or *gwailo*. If the Chinese refer to you by these terms, they may be suspicious of you as someone who is not Chinese.

Advice From the Experts

"When establishing a business relationship, try to find the person who is in a position to make decisions. Otherwise, negotiations will go on indefinitely."

—*Gregory Caraboolad, Chief Tooling Engineer for PMC Industries, a machine tool builder serving the gas and oil industry*

"Eat your food noisily and burp often. Despite what Americans may feel about etiquette, enjoyment of one's meal is perceived differently across the Pacific. Also, offer many toasts by saying, *ganbei* ('bottoms up')."

—*John Balanda, President, Pacific Corporation*

Chapter 3

Hong Kong

---

9 reasons people do business in Hong Kong

1. Hong Kong is a major center for banking and trade.
2. It is closely linked to China with its imports and exports.
3. Its GDP is one of the highest internationally.
4. Hong Kong's shipping ports are among the best internationally.
5. Its major industries include tourism, apparel, textiles, electronics, iron, steel, shipbuilding, fishing, cement, and small manufacturers.
6. The Hong Kong Chinese are a very ambitious group of people.
7. Many people in Hong Kong speak English.
8. Hong Kong has become a leading market in fashion design.
9. Its spinning mills are among the best in the world.

Hong Kong is located at the southeast tip of China and consists of three territories: Hong Kong Island, the Kowloon Peninsula, and the New Territories, as well as 235 islands, largely uninhabited. While Hong Kong Island is approximately 30 square miles, the entire territory covers 413 square miles, and the 235 islands are situated over 1,130 square miles. The largest of these is Lantau, site of the new Chek Lap Kok Airport.

With its strategic location in the center of East Asia, Hong Kong is tailor-made as a gateway for trade and investment between Asia and the rest of the world. For this reason, it is considered to be the world's fastest-growing economic region. It is also the busiest attraction for tourists in the Asia region, with more than 11 million visitors per year. The country boasts a population in excess of six million people.

It is common for residents and visitors to refer to the various parts of Hong Kong in three ways:

1. The Hong Kong side (on the island).

2. Tsuen Wan.

3. The Kowloon side (on the peninsula).

    (Note: Kowloon or *Gow Lung*, means "Nine Dragons" in Chinese.)

Originally a small fishing territory, in the 1800s the British arrived and began using it as a naval base during the Opium Wars. In time, Great Britain gained full control of Hong Kong Island, Kowloon, and finally, the New Territories, which was acquired on a 99-year lease signed with the Chinese in 1898. Over the course of 150 years of British control, Hong Kong became an economic powerhouse in the region, with a large percentage of the population making a living through business developments. In 1984, Great Britain and China signed an agreement that would turn control of the territory back over to the Chinese in 1997, although with the caveat that the territory would retain its commercial and legal autonomy until 2047, at which time, China would once again be able to take full control. This caveat designated Hong Kong as a Special Autonomous Region (SAR) of the People's Republic of China. Its autonomy is upheld by a special mini-constitution devised by the Chinese, called the *Basic Law*.

Statistics and Information

Country Code

Hong Kong's country code is 852.

When you are in Hong Kong and would like to call another country, dial 001, followed by:

- 61 for Australia.
- 86 for China.
- 44 for Great Britain.
- 1 for the United States or Canada.

Currency

Hong Kong operates on the *Hong Kong dollar*. The best way to learn the present currency rate is by checking the local newspapers.

One Hong Kong dollar equals 100 cents. This note is available in six different denominations: 10, 20, 50, 100, 500, and 1,000. The HK$1, 2, and 5 are also available in silver coins.

When exchanging money, go to a bank (such as Hong Kong Bank and Standard Chartered) first, since banks offer the best rates. If they are not open when you would like to exchange currency, your second choice should be a hotel. Last on the list should be money-changers; some may charge in excess of a 5-percent commission.

When exchanging traveler's checks for this country's currency, be sure to have your passport—you will need it for identification.

Ethnic Makeup

Approximately 97 percent of Hong Kong consists of individuals of Chinese descent. The remaining residents have ancestries from the Philippines, Malaysia, Singapore, Japan, Thailand, and Indonesia.

Helpful Hints for Travel

Expect to pay a departure tax of HK$100 at the airport.

When taking a taxi, prepare to pay HK$5 for each piece of luggage.

Make sure that your hand-carried luggage is no larger than 22 inches by 14 inches by 9 inches.

Holidays

The following are the holidays that are celebrated throughout the country. Because these are considered national holidays, it is wise to avoid scheduling meetings during these times.

January 1	New Years Day
Late January/ February	Spring Festival & Chinese New Year (3 days; the dates vary, depending on the lunar calendar)
Spring	Easter
April 5	Ching Ming Festival (an ancestral observance to receive blessings)
May/June	Dragon Boat Festival (commemorates a hero of ancient China: the poet Qu Yuan, who drowned himself in protest against injustice and corruption; the date varies, depending on the lunar calendar)

June 11	While this day used to be celebrated as the Queen's Birthday, China's acquisition of Hong Kong has ended the holiday's official celebration
Last Monday in August	Liberation Day (Tuen Ng)
September/ October	Mid-Autumn Festival (the date varies depending on the lunar calendar)
December 25	Christmas Day
December 26	Boxing Day

Language

The Cantonese dialect of Chinese and English are the predominant languages in Hong Kong. Because it is common for cab drivers not to speak English, it is a good idea to have someone write down your destination and to where you will be returning in Cantonese.

If you hear the term *Xiang Gang*, it is the *putonghua* or Mandarin term for Hong Kong.

Religion

Most Hong Kong Chinese residents practice Buddhism, Taoism, or Confucianism.

Approximately 20 percent of Hong Kong Chinese residents practice Christianity.

Time Zone Differences

Hong Kong is:

- Eight hours ahead of Greenwich Mean Time.
- 13 hours ahead of U.S. Eastern Standard Time.
- Two hours behind Eastern Australian Time.

Note: If you are in Hong Kong and would like to check the time or the temperature, dial 18501.

Weather

Depending on when you will be visiting Hong Kong, the temperature will vary. For example, during the first quarter of the year, it is common for temperatures to be in the 50s and 60s, especially during the second month of the year.

From March through mid-summer, the humidity will increase, with the temperature going as high as the high 70s to the high 80s. During the autumn, the weather is usually warm and sunny. Finally, during the last quarter of the year, you may experience cool, dry, and sunny weather.

If you are in Hong Kong, during the middle of summer, expect to experience *tai-wong* or "Supreme Winds." (This accurately describes the strong winds and rain in Hong Kong, caused by typhoons during July through September.)

Etiquette

Business Attire

When visiting Hong Kong, prepare to dress professionally, in an appropriate business-like manner. The quality of your dress will make a strong impression on the people of Hong Kong. They prefer designer labels and ornate jewelry. Take pride in wearing the finest clothes possible when conducting business. A businesswoman's professional actions and demeanor will be taken as seriously as the business manner in which she is dressed, preferably in a high-quality suit or business dress.

If you receive an invitation that requires a "lounge suit," men should wear a business suit, while women should wear an outfit that is simple yet very elegant. On informal occasions, men should wear a dress shirt with sport coat and trousers.

Business-card Etiquette

To Westerners, business cards are a way of letting others know your mail, phone, fax, and e-mail information. However, to the Hong Kong Chinese, business cards or "name cards" carry a much greater significance, because they assist in developing a relationship between two individuals. Your business card will tell a person from Hong Kong what he or she wants to know about your status and the amount of respect you are to be shown. That is one reason both your title and your organization's logo should be emphasized on the card.

It is very important to go to Hong Kong with an abundance of business cards. If someone offers you a card and you don't reciprocate, the person may interpret this as a sign that you are not interested in developing a business relationship with him or her. In addition, if you are without business cards, you will be perceived as having less credibility.

As soon as you arrive in Hong Kong, if not before, arrange to have your business cards translated into Chinese (using "classical" or "traditional" characters) on the reverse side. Note: Hong Kong and Taiwan are the only countries that still use classical characters rather than the "simplified" ones.

When presenting your business card, present it with both hands so that the receiver can immediately study it rather than having to turn it around to look at it.

When receiving another person's business card, accept it with both hands. Make a point of looking at it for a few moments and of complimenting what you see (the logo, the person's title, etc.).

Be sure that you carry your cards in a card case. Because your cards are representative of you, they should be in excellent condition, rather than tattered or bent.

Business Entertaining/Dining

As with a meeting, the person hosting a banquette will await your arrival. If the guests include several members of your company, you should make a point of having your most senior person enter first, with the rest following in ranking order.

If you are applauded by your hosts, recognize this as a gesture to welcome you. To acknowledge it, applaud them in return.

Prepare for what Westerners consider to be a very lengthy meal, consisting of 10 to 12 courses. You will most likely be seated at a round table with food for each course presented in the middle of the table. Depending upon the situation, either your host or a server will serve you each course, with either a large spoon, a set of chopsticks used exclusively for serving, or the opposite end of the chopsticks he is using to eat.

Instead of receiving a napkin to use throughout the meal, Hong Kong etiquette dictates that you receive a hot towel both before and after the meal. It is appropriate for you to use this towel for your hands and your face.

Be prepared to experience cuisine that you may never have had a chance to taste before. It may include shark's fin soup, abalone, or snake soup (quite a delicacy and very costly). It is considered good manners to eat slowly and to do your best to taste each course. By not doing so, you will risk offending your host.

When fish is served, notice that it will be placed on the table with the fish head facing the guest of honor. This part of the fish is considered quite a delicacy. If you are the guest of honor, you should not move it, but keep it in the position in which it is served to you. If you turn it over, that will be considered bad form.

Rather than deboning the fish yourself, allow either your host or your server to debone it for you.

By Western standards, it is considered gauche to use toothpicks in public. However, it is acceptable by the Hong Kong Chinese to use them between courses in order to dislodge food between your teeth and to pick up food (such as mushrooms) that may be a challenge when using chopsticks.

When eating rice, it is acceptable to take the bowl to your lips and then use your chopsticks to "shovel" the rice into your mouth.

You should leave something on your plate at the end of each course. This will demonstrate that you were satisfied with that course. (If you act as though you are a member of the "Clean Plate

Club" by finishing everything, it may be interpreted that you did not receive enough.)

While Westerners make a point of trying to keep tablecloths from being soiled when eating, in Hong Kong it is acceptable to put fish or chicken bones or the like directly on the tablecloth rather than on an available plate, unless a special plate has been provided to you for discarded bones.

You will know that the meal is nearing an end when you are served fried rice or noodles. It is served for mere form and it is considered appropriate not to touch this course. If you do, it may be misconstrued that the other courses have not satisfied you.

Other ways to know that the meal is nearing an end is when a server places flowers in the middle of the lazy Susan, if fruit is served, and/or if you are handed a finger towel.

While offering to split the bill may be considered a kind gesture in some countries, that is not the case in Hong Kong. Whoever extends the invitation picks up the bill.

If you are hosting a meal, the gesture for letting a server know that you are ready for your bill is by using the universal gesture of raising your hand and pretending you are writing on it.

Chopstick Etiquette

You will be expected to use chopsticks when you are in Hong Kong—and to be proficient with them! Here are some do's and don'ts to help you observe the proper chopstick etiquette:

Do

- Learn in advance to use your chopsticks as well as possible.

- Place your chopsticks on the rest provided to you when you are not using them.

- Lay your chopsticks across each other when you are eating in a dim sum restaurant. This gesture will be a cue to your server that you would like your bill.

Don't

- Ever point with your chopsticks.

- Lay your chopsticks across each other because it is thought to bring bad luck. You may, however, cross chopsticks if you are in a dim sum restaurant and want to gesture that you have completed your meal and would like to take care of the bill. In turn, the server may also cross chopsticks to indicate that the bill has been settled.

- Stick your chopsticks in your rice bowl standing straight up.

Conversation

The citizens of Hong Kong are driven people who value success and who like to display their achievements through their lifestyles. You will be safe in allowing your Hong Kong associate to set the tone of discussion. The safest topics are business, education, and travel. You may also inquire about your Hong Kong client's family.

To Westerners, questions related to age, salary, whether you are married, your personal life, and so on, are considered rude. However, just as in China, these questions are considered acceptable in Hong Kong; therefore, you should be prepared to answer them. The best way to respond is to be indirect, so that you can maintain your privacy and at the same time allow your Hong Kong Chinese contact to save face.

Avoid discussing death, poverty, or defeat. The people of Hong Kong are superstitious and such topics can make them uncomfortable.

While it will be important to know the money that will be at stake in your business dealings, you may never get to that point in the relationship if you approach this topic before it is time to do so. For that reason, leave this topic for last, before you get to the point of signing agreements.

Developing a Business Relationship

Before any kind of business relationship can be established, a personal relationship must be developed first. For that reason, some business relationships can take many years to develop.

It is important for Westerners to realize that it will take both a financial and a time investment to establish a long-term relationship with individuals from Hong King culture. What this means is that two to three trips to Hong Kong may be necessary before business is actually transacted.

Feng Shui

Feng shui (meaning "wind and water") describes an ancient Chinese practice of living in harmony with the land and space around you. This practice emphasizes the importance of energy and its flow. Through this Chinese practice, it is believed the people can control their relationships with their surroundings.

In Hong Kong culture, the *feng shui* is the Chinese person who should be consulted anytime anything is being built or torn down. This individual provides the necessary counsel for determining on which part of the Earth Dragon the structure or object will be laid or built. The *feng shui's* role is also to assist in keeping out evil spirits. It is important to respect the role of the *feng shui* in Hong Kong Chinese culture.

Gestures and Public Manners

Be sure to practice patience rather than haste, and sincerity rather than pretentiousness. Treating others with respect is vital for establishing long-term relationships with the Hong Kong Chinese.

Be mindful of your body language. Looks of disgust, moving around in your chair, pacing, and the like may be interpreted as signs of impatience.

Eye contact does not carry the same importance in Hong Kong as it does in the Western world. Breaking or simply not making eye contact is considered quite appropriate for the Hong Kong Chinese.

Contrary to Western etiquette, smoking is both acceptable and commonplace in Hong Kong. If smoking bothers you, avoid telling others. Instead, do your best to tolerate the smoke; otherwise you may insult your hosts.

If you are a smoker, always offer a cigarette to others before lighting up yourself.

The people of Hong Kong seldom utilize hand motions to emphasize their speech. Therefore, they may be taken aback by some of the grand motions of Westerners. Try to keep your hand and arm movements in check as much as possible.

Always maintain excellent posture when you stand and sit. Slouching can appear disrespectful.

Never allow the soles of your feet to be seen; keep them flat on the floor. This rules out crossing your legs and placing your feet on a desk or chair.

Don't be surprised if your Hong Kong contact stands closer to you than two arm's lengths. While the Hong King Chinese don't like to be physically touched (with the exception of the handshake), standing close together is acceptable and expected.

Don't wink; it is considered to be a rude gesture.

Don't use your finger to point to something. Use your entire hand, palm open.

A wave of the hand in front of the face is a sign for "no."

Gift-giving Etiquette

In addition to entertaining, gift-giving and receiving are important parts of establishing a business rapport. Therefore, bring several gifts with you when you go to Hong Kong.

Gifts such as quality pens, objects commemorating your city, or paperweights with your organization's logo are valued gifts. Because hierarchy and "saving face" are important, it is appropriate to take gifts of different value so that you will be able to give an object of greater quality to a manager and ones of lesser quality to that person's subordinates.

The numbers 3, 8, and 9 are considered lucky numbers and should be kept in mind when selecting gifts to bring with you. The reason is that the Cantonese term for 3 sounds like "life," the term for 8 is similar to the word for "prosperity," and the Chinese word for 9 sounds like "eternity."

Avoid giving gifts in multiples of four. Also avoid giving clocks, because this is considered bad luck. (The word for "clock" sounds like the term for death.) Cutlery or letter openers are also taboo; giving these sorts of gifts may be interpreted as severing ties.

Even if you encourage him or her to do so, don't expect your Chinese contact to open your gift in front of you. When you receive a gift, you may be encouraged more than once to unwrap it. However, it is considered good form to do so in private.

Your gift must be wrapped. The reason is that it will assist the recipient to save face if he or she has given you a lesser gift in return, doesn't care for your gift, or chooses to recycle it (that is, give it to another person) in the future.

Gold and red are the recommended colors for gift wrap. However, red should be avoided when giving flowers or when using a pen.

Reciprocity is very important both in value and quantity. While it may not appear this way, you can be sure that any gift you present or any favor you do for another will be both remembered and reciprocated.

Greetings and Introductions

Be prepared to give and also to receive a lighter handshake than normal. The handshake may be light, but it may also last for a few seconds longer than you are used to receiving.

When making introductions, be sure to introduce the most senior person before presenting the more junior individuals.

Business etiquette dictates that you address your Hong Kong Chinese contacts by their last names (family names), unless asked to do otherwise. Note that if you use a first name, you will risk offending the person.

As per Chinese culture, the last name is put before the first name. For example, a man with the last name of Wong should be addressed as "Wong Sinsang," which is translated as "Mr. Wong."

A married woman should be addressed as "Wong Taaitaai," which is translated as "Mrs. Wong." A single woman should be addressed as "Wong Siuje," which is translated as "Miss Wong."

Hierarchy Is Important

When establishing relationships with the Hong Kong Chinese, recognize that age and rank are important factors. By understanding the impact of these "subcultures" and their roles in society, you will make it easier for others to interact with you.

You should also let the Hong Kong Chinese with whom you are interacting know who the decision-maker is in your organization by deferring respect to your most senior person. If you do not give this type of cue, the Hong Kong Chinese may make an educated guess based on who the eldest person is and also by the most senior title on your business cards.

Meeting Manners

The larger the Hong Kong firm, the farther in advance meetings should be scheduled. Prior to your arrival, send a list of all delegates attending, in ranking order with titles next to each name.

Most likely, the Hong Kong team will be seated and awaiting your arrival. Enter the room in hierarchical order and sit across from the Hong Kong person who holds the position of equal status to your own.

Social conversation will start all meetings and should continue until your Hong Kong Chinese leader moves the talk to business. You will notice that one person, usually a high-ranking officer, will act as the group's spokesperson. Your team should do the same.

Negotiations will be a slow, tedious process. Because a group consensus is the norm in decision-making, you will probably not get a "reading" at the first meeting. The Hong Kong team will want to discuss the proposal in private.

Punctuality

Many Hong Kong Chinese view Westerners as allowing time to control them rather than allowing themselves to flow with time.

Therefore, time management systems are not used with the same gusto as they are by Westerners. Nevertheless, be on time for appointments, even if, as will be likely, your Asian counterparts are up to a half hour late.

Punctuality will be appreciated, but not necessarily expected. If people are late for meetings, it may be because of the heavy traffic that is common in Hong Kong. Therefore, a meeting will probably begin within 30 minutes of the appointed time. Because saving face is very important, it is appropriate to expect this time delay rather than strict punctuality.

Seating Etiquette

Whether you are in a meeting or at a banquet or similar setting, proper seating etiquette should be observed. The seat of honor is the center seat facing the door. The host is seated directly across from the guest of honor, with his or her back to the door.

If you are offered the seat of honor, Hong Kong seating etiquette dictates that you make a gesture or say a word or two to indicate that you are declining the honor. By doing this, you will be perceived as displaying your unworthiness for this honored seat. Immediately accepting it would be perceived as arrogant.

All other attendees should be seated in descending order based on the hierarchical order.

Taxi Etiquette

Although most people speak English in Hong Kong, this may not be the case with all cab drivers. To be on the safe side, ask the hotel concierge to write down your destination in Cantonese. You may also want this person to write down the directions to your hotel for your return ride.

When you get into a cab, be prepared for the radio to be blaring. You may also experience an interesting ride, with the vehicle coming to a screeching halt now and then.

Be prepared for the driver to round out the fare to the closest Hong Kong dollar. For that reason, be sure to have plenty of change with you. By doing so, you can use your discretion to give the cab driver the "extra" rather than risk his keeping more than you are prepared to give.

Tea Etiquette

When you are in a meeting-like setting, you will most likely be served tea. Don't drink it immediately, but wait for the most senior host to take the first sip. Apart from being a refreshment, tea being sipped by a host can be a cue that a meeting is going well. The host not sipping tea can also serve as a cue that the meeting is about to end.

Just as iced tea is consumed with many meals in the West, hot tea is the norm in Hong Kong and other countries that are comprised of primarily Chinese or Japanese individuals. While you will see some British customs in Hong Kong, this will not be the case with tea. Rather than drinking tea with cream and sugar, it is taken plain in Hong Kong.

The sign language for requesting more tea is to either open the lid of the teapot or place the unattached lid on the table upside down.

If tea has just been served to someone and the person receiving the tea taps the table with three fingers of one hand, this is a gesture to thank the server.

It is considered good form to refill other people's teacups.

Just as Westerners meet one another for coffee, taking tea in Hong Kong is a way of life as a social activity. Tea is even used to cure ailments.

If you are invited to *yum cha*, you have been invited to have morning or afternoon tea. When taking part in a *yum cha*, you may notice a lot of finger tapping. This is a lovely ritual that began with an emperor of a Qing Dynasty. One day, when this emperor was visiting South China on an "incognito" inspection, he was having tea with others. When it was his turn to pour the tea, he realized he would reveal his royal status if he didn't pour, so he did it like any commoner. Those who knew him wanted to kneel to thank him, but since this would give away his identity, he asked them instead to tap their index finger and two center fingers on the table. This gesture was meant to signify the bow that they would normally extend to him in his role of emperor. Thus, this finger tapping ritual should be followed anytime tea is served to you as a gesture of appreciation to your host, guest, or server.

Tipping Tips

Tipping is more common in Hong Kong than in many other Asian countries. When paying a bill at a restaurant, keep in mind that most restaurants add a 10-percent service charge. However, it is appropriate to add an additional 5 to 10 percent if the service has been outstanding.

While it is unnecessary, it will be appreciated if you leave a small tip for servers, washroom attendants, and hotel bellboys.

If a cab driver assists you with luggage, a 10-percent tip is apropos.

Doormen and porters should be tipped HK$5 for every item they handle for you.

Toasting Etiquette

While you may not be fluent in Cantonese, you certainly can establish rapport by knowing how to toast the proper way. While most Hong Kong Chinese understand English, it will be very much appreciated if you integrate one of the following phrases into your toasts, based on the situation:

1. For "Cheers," say *"Yum boui."*

2. If you would like to challenge another to consume the entire beverage, say *"Yum sing."*

When you are being toasted, don't feel compelled to drink the entire beverage, especially if it is the second or third alcoholic beverage served to you.

Whether you're the host or the guest, you should be prepared to make a toast. In fact, guests are expected to make toasts.

Take your cue from those hosting the meal. If others stand when a toast is made, you should stand, too.

Guest etiquette dictates that the most senior guest extend a toast toward the end of the meal to give his or her thanks for the evening. This toast should mention the successful long-term relationship that you look forward to having with your Hong Kong Chinese contacts.

When You Are Invited to a Hong Kong Home

The Hong Kong Chinese prefer to entertain at restaurants, banquet halls, or fine hotels. Invitations to a private home are rare. If one is extended to you, you should do your best to accept. Arrive on time and take a small gift that the entire family can appreciate. Follow the lead of your host regarding dinner and post-dinner conversation.

Women in Business

Businesswomen in Hong Kong enjoy some of the best, most equal treatment in all of Asia. Just the same, you should conduct yourself in a professional manner and stay focused on your task. This will dispel any rare attempts to make you feel uncomfortable.

Whatever You Do...

- Don't run out of business cards. Not giving a card to another may be interpreted as not wanting to establish a business relationship with the person.

- Don't wink, chew gum, or blow your nose in public. These gestures are considered offensive.

- Don't be afraid to belch or slurp soup or noodles when eating. Making noises when eating is considered a sign that you are satisfied.

- Don't be afraid to use toothpicks after eating. Unlike Western manners, this gesture is considered acceptable at the table as long as you hold your hand in front of your mouth.

- Don't put your hands on your lap when sitting or behind your back when standing. Hands should be showing at all times.

- Don't wear slacks if you are a woman. Business suits, skirts and blouses, or dresses are more appropriate.

- Don't acknowledge a compliment by thanking the person. Display your humility instead by declining the kind words. You should also expect this type of behavior when paying a compliment to the Hong Kong Chinese.

- Don't take a photo of someone without first asking permission.

- Don't give white flowers to your host. This color symbolizes mourning to the Hong Kong Chinese.

- Don't give anything in the shape of a triangle, because this form is thought to signify bad luck.

Advice From the Experts

"Shake hands...Bow your head...Exchange your business card so that it is right side up to the recipient...drink very moderately...tip 10 percent."

—*James O. Newman, President, Newman Leather Corporation*

Chapter 4

Indonesia

7 reasons people do business in Indonesia

1. Indonesia receives the most imported products from Japan, the United States, and Germany.

2. Indonesia exports the most products to Japan, the United States, and Singapore.

3. Its location is ideal for export throughout Asia and across the globe.

4. Indonesia's potential market is too vast to ignore.

5. The country is known for its low production costs.

6. Indonesia is known for its food processing, textile, cement, and light industries.

7. Indonesia is a major grower of crops that include rice, cocoa, and peanuts. It is also rich in resources such as nickel, tin, oil, bauxite, copper, and gas.

The nation of Indonesia is an archipelago composed of more than 17,000 islands spread between the continents of Australia and Asia in the Indian and Pacific Oceans. Only 6,000 of the islands are inhabited, the main ones being Sumatra, Kalimantan (shared with Malaysia), Selawesi, Irian Jaya (shared with Papua New Guinea), and Java. The capital is Jakarta, located on the north coast of Java. With more than 200 million inhabitants, Indonesia is the world's fourth most populous country, as well as the largest archipelago, with land area totaling 782,655 square miles. There is a vast array of landscapes and natural resources, with more than half of the land mass protected as natural wilderness.

Approximately 300 different ethnic groups inhabit the islands, making the country tremendously multicultural. At one time one of the world's poorest countries, Indonesia (which has been a strategically important country in world trade for centuries) is now a thriving developing nation, having experienced solid economic growth and political stability within the last 50 years. For more than 350 years, the archipelago was controlled by the Dutch, until Japan occupied the country in 1942. An underground resistance force fought to achieve independence for Indonesia, which was granted in 1945, at which time a representational government was formed. The underground's leader, Soekarno, became the nation's first president. He was succeeded by Soeharto in 1965, after many years of rebellions and attempted Communist coups. Soeharto created the economic initiatives that turned Indonesia into the vibrant and important country it is today. It is a close ally to the United States, with which it maintains strong economic ties.

Statistics and Information

Air Travel

The official name of the Jakarta airport is Jakarta Soekahno Hatta International Airport.

The easiest way to get to a hotel in Jakarta, Surabaya, or Bandung, which are all on the island of Java, is either by cab or bus. If you have a lot of luggage or have traveled a long distance, a taxi is highly recommended. The same type of transportation applies when traveling to cities such as Medan on the island of Sumatra.

Country Code

The country code for Indonesia is 62.

Major city codes include:

- 542 for Balikpapan.
- 21 for Jakarta.
- 431 for Manado.
- 61 for Medan.
- 751 for Padang.
- 711 for Palembang.
- 31 for Surabaya.
- 283 for Tegal.

Currency

Indonesia's currency is the *rupiah*. One *rupiah* (Rp) = 100 *sen*. Bills come in denominations of 10,000, 5,000, 1,000, 500, and 100 Rp. Coins come in 100, 50, and 25 Rp.

Contrary to what you will find when doing business in Hong Kong, the best place to exchange money in Indonesia is through licensed money-changers. Banks and hotels tend to give lower exchange rates. On the other hand, while you will get the best rates when exchanging U.S. dollars with money-changers, you may do better at banks with currencies from other countries.

When exchanging traveler's checks for this country's currency, be sure to have your passport—you will need it for identification.

Dates

When writing dates, be sure to indicate the day first, followed by the month, and then the year. For example, May 4, 1999, should be written as 4/5/99.

Ethnic Makeup

As the fourth most populous nation in the world, Indonesia's people represent a great variety of ethnic backgrounds. About half of the population is Javanese, with more than 10 percent Sudanese, approximately 14 percent Madurese, and 7.5 percent Coastal Malays. The remainder is comprised of nearly 300 different ethnicities.

Holidays

The following are the holidays that are celebrated throughout Indonesia and in specific sections of the country. Therefore, it is wise to avoid scheduling meetings during these times.

January 1	New Year's Day
Late January/ Early February *	Mi'naj Nabi Muhammad (The Ascension of Muhammad)
Late February/ Early March *	Ramadan
Late March *	Nyepi (a Hindu holiday celebrated throughout the country; Bali observes this holiday in silence)
Late March/ Early April *	Good Friday
Late March/ Early April *	Easter

May 21	Waisaki (the anniversary of the birth and death of Buddha)
July *	Haji (the celebration of the Mecca pilgrimages)
August 17	Independence Day
August *	Maulid Nabi (Muhammad's birthday)
December 25	Christmas Day

* These holidays vary widely, based on the lunar calendar.

Also, note that many people of the upper class travel abroad in the months of July and August, therefore the company decision-makers may be gone during this time.

Language

The country's official language is Bahasa Indonesian, which is a modified form of Malay. Although you will hear more than 300 different languages spoken, Javanese is the second most commonly spoken language. You will also hear Dutch and English spoken frequently.

Religion

Indonesia has the largest Sunni Muslim population in the world, with just under 90 percent of Indonesians practicing this religion. Approximately 6 percent of the population practices Christianity (mostly Protestantism and Catholicism). Less than 5 percent of Indonesians practice Buddhism, Hinduism, and Confucianism.

Time Zone Differences

There are three time zones in Indonesia:

- *Western Indonesian Time,* which is seven hours ahead of Greenwich Mean Time and 12 hours ahead of U.S. Eastern Standard Time. Java, Sumatra, and West and Central Kalimantan are in this time zone.

- *Central Indonesian Time*, which is eight hours ahead of Greenwich Mean Time and 13 hours ahead of U.S. Eastern Standard Time. Bali, West and East Nusatenggara, and East Timor are in this time zone.
- *East Indonesian Time,* which is nine hours ahead of Greenwich Mean Time and 14 hours ahead of U.S. Eastern Standard Time. Maluku and Irian Jaya are in this time zone.

Weather

Humidity in this tropical climate ranges from 70 to 100 percent all year. Temperatures range from the low 70s to the mid-90s. Rain is abundant from November to April, with the greatest precipitation in December and January.

Etiquette

Business Attire

Indonesia is predominantly a Muslim culture, so conservative dress is key. Western-style suits are worn by most Indonesian business professionals, especially during very formal meetings with high-ranking dignitaries. During less formal gatherings, a shirt and tie is acceptable. When in doubt, it is best to err on the side of conservatism.

Because of the intense humidity, clothes made of natural fibers work best. Just as in many other Asian countries, women should wear skirted suits or business dresses with sleeves and hems that are conservative in length. Bright rather than dark colors should be worn. Women should avoid wearing slacks.

Business-card Etiquette

When meeting a new associate, the exchange of business cards should be done immediately after the initial handshake and greeting. The proper way to continue the introduction is by offering your business card with your right hand, facing the recipient.

When you receive another person's business card, do so with two hands. Be sure to study it for a few moments before carefully putting it into your card case or laying it on the table nearest you.

Indonesians appreciate ornate cards. Therefore make a point of having your business card printed in color with embossing, when possible. Although presenting your business card in English is acceptable, you may want to go that extra mile by having your cards translated on the reverse side. Be sure your card emphasizes your name and position.

Business Entertaining/Dining

Indonesians view personal relationships as key to developing business relationships, so time should be spent on social engagements. They will look favorably on any invitations to post-business functions, as well as your acceptance of their invitations. However, remember to keep this strictly social. Do not bring up business unless your Indonesian counterparts initiate such talk.

Spouses may be included in any invitations.

Whoever extends the invitation is responsible for taking care of the bill. If you receive invitations during your stay, be sure to reciprocate before returning home.

Always familiarize yourself with the most senior person present. This individual should be considered the guest of honor at a meal. You should demonstrate respect for this person by waiting until he has ordered before you do so. Additionally, wait until he has served himself and has taken the first sip of his beverage before you follow suit.

You will be presented with a wide array of food originating in Indonesia's numerous regions. Try your best to sample everything, if for no other reason than as a sign of respect for the Indonesian culture.

Seasonings are an essential part of Indonesian cooking. In fact, many of the seasonings taste hot and spicy rather than mild. For this reason alone, be sure to have sufficient beverages to drink.

Rice will be served at every meal and combined with a variety of meats and vegetables. Some cuisine unknown to Westerners includes shrimp served (and eaten) with the legs still attached, fish-head soup, buffalo, and goat meat. One costly delicacy that you may have the chance to sample is live monkey brains. Brace yourself if your host does select this, as the monkey's head will be strapped in the middle of the table.

When eating, be sure to use the fork and spoon. Place your fork in your left hand with your spoon in your right hand. Use your fork for pushing food onto the spoon.

Always leave a portion of your meal on your plate to show that you've been satisfied with the meal.

When you have finished your meal, place your fork with the tines down on your plate and cross the spoon over it.

Conversation

You should feel free to broach a wide range of subjects with your Indonesian friends. Sports, travel, family, and the weather are always safe topics of conversation. Because the Indonesian government places great emphasis on fitness and recreation, inquiring about a person's interests in physical pursuits may ignite a lively discussion.

Do not discuss any topics that may imply criticism of the Indonesian culture or lifestyle. Also avoid talking about religion, politics, or any social customs that you find unusual compared to your own culture.

There is a belief in Indonesia that the office is the only place to discuss business. Therefore, make a point of not discussing business proceedings or deal-making in a social situation.

Gestures and Public Manners

Don't be surprised if you see members of the same sex walking hand-in-hand or arm-in-arm. This simply conveys their high level of comfort and friendship.

Touching between males and females should be avoided in public.

Avoid prolonged periods of eye contact, because this may cause Indonesians to feel uncomfortable.

When traveling by bus, men are expected to give their seats to women, and younger people should do the same for older people. If you are seated, don't be surprised if you are approached by a person who is standing and carrying a package to ask if you would hold the package because you are seated.

Because of the typical Indonesian's lack of public emotion, quiet voice, and contained gestures, this nationality is often perceived as shy. On the contrary, this culture simply believes that a more restrained and controlled public appearance gains respect. Indonesians are very subtle in their interactions, yet they are keen to the behavior of others. Use discretion in your public displays. Also, make a point of not raising your voice or expressing anger.

Here are six gesture "don'ts" to keep in mind when interacting with Indonesians:

1. Don't use your left hand for eating, touching another person, or even motioning to someone else.

2. Don't touch anyone on the head. This part of the body is thought to contain the spirit of the person and is sacred. This includes children.

3. Don't allow the soles of your feet to show. Make sure your feet face the ground and your legs remain uncrossed.

4. Don't point using your forefinger. Instead, use your thumb and place the rest of your fingers in a fist.

5. Don't motion for someone to come near you by waving with your palm up and facing you. Instead, use your entire hand, palm down, in a scooping motion towards you

6. Don't place your hands in your pockets, on your hips, or across your chest. These gestures may be seen as non-verbal acts of aggression or defiance.

Gift-giving Etiquette

One of the best ways to demonstrate your interest and sincerity in establishing a long-standing personal and business relationship is to present your Indonesian associates with gifts during your first meeting. The items you select need not be fancy, just tokens from your country or objects with your company's logo.

Expect gifts to be refused the first couple of times you present them. However, be persistent, since the person will accept them eventually.

Your gift will not be opened in front of you and words of thanks are not part of the process. However, rest assured that the recipient will comment about your act of kindness because of the gift you presented to him or her. Conversely, do not open any gifts you receive in front of the giver.

When giving a gift to Muslims, avoid alcohol or anything to do with pigs or dogs. When giving a gift to Hindus, do not present anything made of leather.

Greetings and Introductions

Interactions with business associates in Indonesia should be formal and done in a respectful manner. The proper greeting includes bowing your head, lowering your eyes, and smiling while giving the Indonesian a greeting such as *"Selamat,"* which is translated as "peace."

Handshakes should be lighter than most Westerners are used to giving and receiving. Handshakes should also be held for a longer period of time than it takes to greet the person. During subsequent meetings with Indonesians, it is appropriate to bow rather than repeat handshakes.

Indonesian names also are considered sacred and reflect the status of a family. Names are said and also written in Western order (first name followed by the family name). They may be several syllables longer than most people are used to hearing or pronouncing. When you are unsure about how to pronounce a name, ask the Indonesian person with whom you are meeting for assistance with proper pronunciation. Many Indonesians have shortened versions of their names for general use and this person may suggest that you address him or her in this fashion.

The use of last names is essential and should be used unless you are specifically invited to use a less formal address. If the person has a professional title, such as doctor, professor, or the like, it should be placed before the last name. Otherwise, the titles of, for example, "Mr. Bapak" and "Madame Ibu" are sufficient.

Meeting Manners

Meetings are more formal in Indonesia than in many other Asian countries. Typically, Indonesian businesspeople will enter the room based on their hierarchical position and take a seat. When you are involved in a meeting, be sure to remain standing until this procedure has taken place.

Although the meeting will probably begin with a bit of small talk, be prepared to get down to business soon after tea has been served.

It will be in your best interest to have your presentation material and company literature translated into Bahasa.

When establishing business relationships with Indonesians, be patient and diligent. Indonesian businesspeople are slow and deliberate when it comes to making decisions. If you attempt to rush them through the negotiation process, you risk being regarded unfavorably. Always remember that a more low-keyed, thoughtful appeal will assist you in maintaining harmony with the individuals across the table from you.

If the Indonesians with whom you are meeting make few comments, don't view their silence as a negative response. Frequently, part of the business practice in this country is to remain aloof until a group meeting can be held to gather a consensus. In addition, remember that these people are naturally soft-spoken, so be aware of your tone of voice and avoid being too loud or harsh-sounding.

Indonesians are shrewd negotiators and come to the bargaining table with the intention of leaving with the best deal possible. Don't be discouraged by what you may consider their apparent lack of responsiveness; just remain positive and persistent. Indonesians respect these qualities and look for business partners who are interested in developing long-term relationships.

Like the country's society, Indonesian business is hierarchical and decision-making lies with senior management. Be sure you are meeting with top officers, especially when a deal reaches the final stages.

Punctuality

Familiarize yourself with the phrase *"jam karet,"* which means "rubber time." This saying is an apology for many mistakes, and is most commonly used when an Indonesian arrives late for a scheduled appointment. You will find that this nationality has a carefree attitude toward time and frequently may be as late as two hours for meetings. Time is not viewed as such a valuable asset, and business is conducted in a much more relaxed manner than in the West.

On the other hand, it is important to recognize the role that hierarchy plays in punctuality. A junior must never be late for a meeting with a superior. In fact, many Indonesians actually time their arrival based on their position. A high-ranking officer will intentionally arrive once he or she knows that all of his or her subordinates have arrived.

Individuals from abroad traveling to Indonesia should not adopt this lax attitude toward time. Instead, they should arrive for appointments based on the scheduled time and simply expect to wait.

Seating Etiquette

Don't be surprised if men and women are seated at separate tables while dining. This is a Muslim custom.

The guest of honor is usually seated next to the host (if the person is a male) or hostess (if the person is a female).

Tipping Tips

When you take a taxi, be sure to negotiate the fare before getting into the cab. Tip at your discretion, but 5- to 10-percent tips, or a minimum of Rp 300 are common. Note that not all taxis are air-conditioned. For short rides you may not mind; however, Indonesia's humidity and high temperatures may encourage you to arrange for a taxi that is air-conditioned. While it may be a few more cents per mile, it will be well worth it.

When you hire a car for the day, be sure to tip the driver. A minimum of Rp 2,000 should be offered.

In many of Indonesia's better restaurants, a 10-percent gratuity charge is added. Be sure to check the bill for this or ask if it has been done. If it hasn't been included, a 10-percent tip should be left.

When bellboys and doormen are of assistance to you, it is in order to tip them approximately Rp 2,000. When you are assisted with your luggage, you should give Rp 500 per bag to the porter.

When You Are Invited to an Indonesian Home

Home invitations are rare because of cramped housing often inhabited by several extended family members. If you are extended an invitation to an associate's home, you should accept, as it is an honor.

Guest etiquette dictates that you arrive 10 to 20 minutes late. Upon arrival, discretely check to see if your host or his or her spouse is wearing shoes. If not, be sure to remove your own shoes.

It is appropriate to bring a gift with you. While any small item will be appreciated, such as sweets or something commemorative of your country, avoid giving alcohol if your hosts are Muslim.

Wait for the host to invite you to begin eating. In the less formal home setting, Indonesians may eat with only the right hand. Forks and spoons should be provided, so feel free to eat with them if you are more comfortable. Just remember, whether or not you use utensils to eat, avoid using your left hand at all costs.

Most Indonesians retire early, so be sure not to overextend your stay and leave at an appropriate hour.

Women in Business

Women traveling to Indonesia will find few or no problems in being accepted as professional businesspeople. Because a large percentage of Indonesian women work outside the home, the culture is accustomed to dealing with professional women. However, it is a good idea to conduct yourself in a conservative manner and not be too aggressive. Women should also be sure to include spouses when extending any invitations for social functions to Indonesian businessmen.

Whatever You Do...

- Don't be late for an appointment, even though your Indonesian associate may be as much as two hours late.

- Don't use your left hand for anything in public. This hand is for use in the bathroom and is considered unclean.

- Don't mispronounce the names of your Indonesian friends. Most Indonesian names are multisyllabic. Therefore, take time to learn their correct pronunciations. Names are sacred in Indonesia and must be treated with respect.

- Don't rush business proceedings. The concept of "rubber time" exists in Indonesia. For that reason, time is not of the utmost importance. Strong personal relationships lead to good business relationships, and those take time to establish.

- Don't be afraid to "haggle" over a business deal. Indonesians bargain for most purchases and exchanges in everyday life and are quite astute in their dealings. For that reason alone, don't confuse a person's reserved demeanor for a lack of business savvy.

- Don't be shocked by the open discussion of birth control. The Indonesian government has initiated a huge campaign to limit the number of children in a family. Consequently, contraception is advertised and promoted openly.

- Don't chew gum in public.

- Don't expect a knife to be part of your dining experience. Only a spoon and fork will be offered.

- Don't write dates the way it's done in the United States. Instead, write the day first, followed by the month, then the year.

Chapter 5

Japan

8 reasons people do business in Japan

1. Japan welcomes businesspeople from abroad.

2. Once Japanese businesspeople make a decision, they are honor-bound. Therefore, the decision is long-lasting.

3. The Japanese tend to be highly motivated, resourceful, and very industrious.

4. Japan covers a variety of industries.

5. This country is very open to receiving imported products.

6. The Japanese are world leaders in the manufacture of electrical and electronic equipment.

7. They are top producers of vehicles, machinery, and chemicals, and they are leaders in the fishing industry.

8. They take pride in delivering high-quality products.

The country of Japan is a chain of islands located between the North Pacific Ocean and the Sea of Japan, east of Korea. With a total land mass of more than 145,800 square miles, it consists of four large islands—Hokkaido, Honshu, Kyushu, and Shikoku—and a number of smaller islands. About the size of California, the country is dotted with several volcanic mountain ranges and is prone to frequent geologic activity. The capital city is Tokyo, one of the most populous cities in the world, as well as an epicenter for trade and development in Southeast Asia.

Respect, honor, courtesy, patience. These are four words that describe the people of Japan. For many centuries, Japan maintained strong links to the Asian mainland and borrowed freely from Chinese culture. In time, however, its people started developing autonomous cultural characteristics. Powerful families ruled various regions of the country until unification was achieved in the late 1500s, after which a prolonged period of isolation from the rest of the world set in. By the mid-1800s, Japan's leaders began to open the country to Western influences, and in time embarked on an imperialistic drive for power and dominion over other countries. This culminated in the 1900s with its invasion of Manchuria and its attack on Pearl Harbor in the United States. The country's defeat in World War II led to a change in how Japan was governed, along with demilitarization, a new constitution, and new economic policies. By the 1970s, Japan had become a leader in world trade and business, a status it maintains today as one of the most influential and important countries in the world.

Statistics and Information

Air Travel

Tokyo's International Airport is located more than an hour away from the heart of the city. Airport limousine buses are the most cost-effective way to reach Tokyo. They leave every quarter of an hour and allow you to have a lot of luggage. If you opt for a taxi, get your checkbook out, because the fare can be as much as $400!

Bullet Train

If you will be traveling between cities in Japan, you will probably take the bullet train, or *Shinkansen*. This form of transportation first became available in 1964. Different cars have different amenities, some with telephones, some with restaurant and dining facilities. There is even a first class or "green car."

When you are traveling on the bullet train, you may get hungry. One way to satisfy your hunger is to enjoy a box lunch that is available to you at each train station. Frequently, the lunch will include a food for which that the particular area of Japan is known.

Country Code

Japan's country code is 81.

Major city codes are:

- 052 for Nagoya.
- 06 for Osaka.
- 03 for Tokyo.

If you are in Japan and are calling another city within the country, you will not need to dial zero.

Currency

Japanese currency is called the *yen* (Y).

For exchanging currency, look for signs saying "Authorized Foreign Exchange Bank." You can also exchange money in hotels and some stores.

When exchanging traveler's checks for this country's currency, be sure to have your passport—you will need it for identification.

Dates

The Japanese corporate world uses the same format as that of the West. Dates are written as month, date, year. January 30, 1999, would be written 1/30/99.

Ethnic Makeup

Japan's population of well over 125 million consists mostly of a single ethnic group of Mongoloid origin, with the addition of a number of minority groups. Approximately three quarters of the population are of Korean descent.

The people of Japan are known for their rigorous work ethic, considered by many to be unique in the world. They recognize the importance of teamwork, how conformity equates to consistency, and the importance of *wa* or harmony.

Holidays

The following are the holidays that are celebrated throughout the country. Because these are considered national holidays, it is wise to avoid scheduling meetings during these times.

January 1	New Year's Day
January 15	Adulthood Day
February 11	Founding of the Nation Day
March 20/21	Vernal Equinox Day (the date varies, depending on the lunar calendar)
April 29	Emperor's Birthday (Greenery Day)
May 3	Constitution Memorial Day

May 5	Children's Day
June 22	Summer Solstice Day
Mid-August	Obon Festival (a religious celebration; also celebrated in July in some cities)
September 15	Respect for the Aged Day
September 23/24	Autumn Equinox Day (the date varies, depending on the lunar calendar)
October 10	Health and Sports Day
November 3	Culture Day
November 23	Labor Thanksgiving Day
December 31	New Year's Eve

Language

Japan's official language is Japanese. English is a widely spoken second language. Although a large majority of the population know how to read and write English, some are less proficient in speaking and understanding the language. For that reason alone, it is wise to have written documentation of what you are going to present or a question you may have for another. By doing so, you will make it easy for your Japanese associates to better understand you.

Religion

The religion that is practiced by the majority of the population is Shintoism, followed by Buddhism. Some people even practice both religions and many practice Christianity. Rather than expressing their beliefs publicly, many Japanese have places of worship (altars) in their own homes.

Time Zone Differences

Japan is nine hours ahead of Greenwich Mean Time and 14 hours ahead of U.S. Eastern Standard Time.

Weather

The temperature and weather you experience in Japan will depend on the time of year that you visit—for instance, spring weather between March and May and autumn weather between September and November, with temperatures ranging from the mid-50s (Fahrenheit) to the mid-60s.

Although on average the climate tends to be moderate, the months of July through September are usually very hot and humid, with temperatures reaching the high 90s.

June and July are typically rainy, so be sure to take an umbrella if you go to Japan in those months.

Etiquette

Bowing

The Japanese bow or *ojiga* is done for many reasons. A bow can be a way of greeting someone, acknowledging an individual, thanking a person, displaying gratitude, saying "I'm sorry," or even asking for a favor.

The Japanese will shake hands with Westerners as a way of making others feel comfortable. Westerners should extend the same courtesy by bowing to acknowledge that they have made an effort to learn the Japanese way. A gesture as small as this can assist in establishing rapport with a potential Japanese client.

When bowing to individuals who are on the same status level as you, you should bow at the same height.

When bowing to someone who is higher than you on the hierarchical level, bow a little lower than that person to display corporate deference.

When bowing to a person and you are uncertain where you fit in with that person on the hierarchy level, always be conservative by bowing slightly lower than that individual.

Just as "the customer is always right" in Western terms, the customer is the person to whom you bow lower in Japanese terms.

When bowing, eyes should be lowered rather than looking at the person. Men should keep their hands at their sides while women should keep their hands in front of them.

Business Attire

Appropriate dress in Japan tends to be conservative. For men, that means suits, and for women business suits and dresses. If your company dresses business casual, leave those clothes at home and count on dressing in more formal business attire.

Because you may be taking your shoes off in some offices, restaurants, temples, and homes, it is a smart idea to wear shoes that can be taken off easily, rather than shoes that tie. Keep in mind that your socks will be seen more than usual, so take care in packing clean and conservative socks. Note: Women should have a pair of footies close at hand for slipping on over hosiery or bare feet.

Business-card (or Meishi) Etiquette

When business cards (called *meishi* in Japan) are exchanged, it is the first step in establishing a relationship. Business cards are a reflection of both the individual and the organization being represented. For that reason, a *meishi* should be treated with the utmost respect.

It is wise to take plenty of business cards with you, because you will be exchanging them with everyone who will be involved in the meetings you will be attending.

Business-card etiquette dictates that you initiate the exchange if you are the person visiting, rather than hosting, the meeting.

When you receive another person's *meishi*, be sure to study it a few seconds before putting it down. Then either lay it on the table if you are sitting or place it in your business card case if you are standing.

Make a point of having your business card translated into Japanese by asking the concierge to do it when you check into your hotel.

Remember that business cards should be treated with the greatest respect. Therefore, be sure not to write on a card or request another card if you are meeting with a person for a second time.

Business Entertaining/Dining

The Japanese love to have a good time and entertaining is almost nightly. When you're in Japan on business, therefore, plan on staying out until the wee hours of the morning.

When you are dining out in a restaurant and you find it necessary to excuse yourself from the table, try to bend at the same height that people are sitting as you are passing by them. This is an important gesture of respect.

If you cannot read the Japanese menu, don't worry. You will be able to decide what you would like to eat from the plastic samples that may be showcased as you enter the restaurant.

A standard Japanese meal consists of a main food (such as grilled fish), a bowl of rice, a cup of soup, and a little dish containing pickles.

Unusual dishes: Be prepared to taste foods that you may never have had a chance to try in your own country. These foods include *inoshishi* or wild boar, *sakura-nabe* or horse meat, *suzume* or sparrow, *uzura* or quail, and *shika-no-shashimi* or raw deer meat.

Just as in many countries, it is appropriate for the host to take the first bite as a signal that the others may begin eating.

It is common for many small dishes to be served during a meal rather than one entree per person, so take care to eat only "your" portion of each dish, based on the number of people who are seated at your table.

Rather than passing up food, you should make an effort to eat a small portion. If you absolutely cannot eat it, rather than saying that you don't like something, it is more appropriate to say that you are unable to eat it "for health reasons." This will allow both you and the Japanese individuals at your table to "save face."

While slurping one's soup or drink is considered rude in many countries, it is quite acceptable in Japan.

One way to indicate that you have finished eating something is by placing the lid back on the bowl.

The appropriate way to handle fish or chicken bones is to place them on the side of your plate, rather than on the tablecloth, which is considered acceptable in some Asian countries.

When you are full, leave some food on your plate, or leave some rice in your bowl. This tells others that you are content and do not want be served more.

You will know that the meal is nearing an end when tea (brown or green) is served.

When drinking soup and other liquids, it is appropriate to lift the bowl and take it directly to your mouth

Never replenish your own beverage; this is considered rude. Instead, wait for another person to fill your glass. When you are drinking a beverage, keep your eye on the beverages of those around you. When you see they need to be replenished, be sure to refill their glasses, rather than waiting for them to do so.

If you are drinking something and don't care for it anymore, simply don't drink it. If you do drink it, the beverage will automatically be refilled.

What to do in a karaoke bar: Although the Japanese work hard, they play just as hard—and that includes when they are in a karaoke bar! This experience is a great way to establish rapport or bond with your potential clients. Whether you can sing or not, you can be certain that you will be on center stage as you are singing or doing a pantomime to either a Japanese or a Western song.

Chopstick Etiquette

If you have traveled to other Asian countries, you may be surprised to find that chopsticks used by the Japanese are actually shorter than those used by the Chinese.

Proper chopstick manners include maintaining good posture and bringing the chopsticks up to your mouth, rather than leaning in to the table and bringing your mouth down to the chopsticks.

Chopsticks have many purposes. Besides being used for picking up food and taking it to your mouth, these utensils also may be used for cutting food into smaller, more manageable pieces.

When you have finished using your chopsticks, they should be placed on the chopstick rest that you will find on the table. They can also be placed on the rest if you are still eating but resting between bites. Do *not* stick your chopsticks straight up and down in the rice bowl.

Conversation

Rather than initiating a conversation, let your Japanese contact set the tone by starting it.

Humility is very important in Japan. Therefore, don't be surprised if the person you are complimenting does not accept your flattering words graciously; they have to show humility by indicating that they may be unworthy of such praise.

Don't be surprised if you are asked questions that may be considered unacceptable in your country, such as:

- "How old are you?"
- "Are you married?"
- "Do you have children?"
- "How much do you weigh?"

Rather than feeling obliged to answer these questions, you can avoid answering by being slightly evasive with your response.

Be careful not to ask questions that may be misinterpreted. For instance, if you would like to attend a Sumo wrestling match and ask where you can purchase tickets, your Japanese contact may misinterpret your questions as a hint that you want him or her to get tickets for you.

Avoid talking about World War II with any Japanese person.

Four Key Ways to Recognize the Highest-ranking Person

1. This person's business card may be presented by one of his subordinates.

2. This individual may pick up his tea to drink it first.

3. This person may appear to be the most quiet of everyone present.

4. This person may not say anything until the end of the meeting.

Gestures, Public Manners, and Other Things to Know

When motioning for someone to "come here," place your *palms down* rather than up and move your fingers towards your body.

When pointing to yourself, point your forefinger towards your nose.

If you want to display that you are ashamed or embarrassed, rub or scratch the back of your head or neck.

When you want your Japanese colleague to know that you are listening to what he or she is saying and understand what is being said, a nod is the gesture to use.

In order to indicate "no," move your hand back and forth in front of your face.

Just as in many other Asian countries, a smile is more than a gesture of happiness. To the Japanese, a smile can express embarrassment or nervousness.

It is considered inappropriate to blow your nose in front of others.

Avoid eating while you are walking down a street; also, don't chew gum in public.

It is considered inappropriate to touch or pat another person on the back.

Refrain from putting your feet on a chair or table, or using your foot to move an object or open and close a door.

Taxis: Your hotel concierge will probably be fluent in English; however, many taxi drivers will not be. Therefore, request that the concierge write down your destination for you and give you the address of your hotel in Japanese.

Toilets: Squat toilets are common in offices, homes, and some restaurants, so be prepared by wearing appropriate clothes for this stance. You also may want to take tissue paper so that you are not caught off guard.

Gift-giving Etiquette

Gift-giving is a common and expected gesture when meeting for the first time. By giving a gift that is representative of your city (such as a classic souvenir with an emblem or logo), you will be establishing rapport the Japanese way.

When you are given a gift and would like to reciprocate, be sure to select an item that is no more than one-third to one half the value of the gift presented to you.

When possible, try to add a personal touch to this gift-giving experience by making a point of presenting the gift personally, rather than having it sent.

Just as with business cards, when giving a gift or receiving one, be sure you do so with both hands.

When you receive a gift, wait until you are alone to open it.

The way a present is wrapped is as important as the gift itself. Consult with the hotel concierge for assistance in wrapping. If you choose to wrap it yourself, choose a light-colored paper. Avoid using black, gray, or white wrapping paper, as well as fancy bows.

If you are working in Japan, note that gifts are given the two times of the year when bonuses are given: during mid-summer (*osiebo*) and at the end of the year (*o-chugen*).

If you work in Japan, when you travel to another country, you will be expected to return with gifts for your fellow workers. What you give them will not be as important as your thoughtfulness.

When choosing a gift, avoid giving anything that has any association with the number 4, which is considered to be an unlucky number (as is 9). Also, do not give gifts in multiples of four. The Japanese feel so strongly about this that not even hospital rooms are numbered with a "4."

When visiting someone in a hospital, it is considered a nice gesture to take fruit or a bouquet of flowers. However, be sure not to take lilies, lotus blossoms, or camellias, because they are associated with funerals. It also is considered bad luck to take a potted plant. The superstition is that a plant in a pot will encourage a sickness to have deeper roots.

Greetings and Introductions

Western cultures expect a firm handshake, but this is not the case in Japan. Use a lighter grip and let go of the other person's hand much sooner than you would if you were shaking hands with someone from another country. Also, be sure to stand a minimum of two arm's lengths from the person.

Your greeting should include a "How do you do," followed by your name, title, and company.

When addressing another person by name, the last name or family name should always be used, preceded by "Mr.," "Mrs.," or "Miss." You might want to make the effort to do it the Japanese way, which is to address the person by his or her last name, followed by *san*—the equivalent of "Mr.," "Mrs.," and "Miss." For example, Mr. Shioda would be Shioda *san*.

If someone is a very high-ranking individual in a company, that person should be addressed by his or her title rather than by the last name. For instance, a general manager whose last name is "Tanaka" would not be addressed as "Tanaka *san*." Instead, the term, "General Manager" or *Bucho* would be used followed by *san*, or *Bucho-san*, followed by the company the person represents. For example, "This is *Bucho-san* of Toshiba, a business associate of Mr. Arnold."

(See also Bowing and Business-card Etiquette.)

How Decisions Are Made

In Japan, business decisions are generally made by groups rather than by individuals. Decisions are made based on harmony (or *wa*) and the majority rule. Once the majority of people have come to an agreement, a document is passed around for each of these individuals to acknowledge their approval with an actual "seal of approval."

Business decisions can take anywhere from one to three years, so patience is a virtue that must be learned when establishing relationships with the Japanese.

Although contracts will be put in writing when decisions are made, the Japanese value trust much more than the piece of paper on which an agreement is written.

Meeting Manners

Seating etiquette: Sit directly across from the individuals with whom you are meeting; the most important person should be in the center, facing the door, and the people on each side of him or her should be facing their counterparts.

A customary Japanese meeting begins with small talk to establish a rapport first. Take the cue from your Japanese customers to know when it is time to begin discussing business.

It is important that you clarify what you are going to present by putting it in writing beforehand, so that everyone will have this information in front of them. It also will be appreciated if you use a pointer, board, or slide presentation to assist your potential customers in following along. Be sure to take notes when business is discussed by others.

"Yes" phrases that may mean "no":

• "We will think about it."

• "We will see."

• "Perhaps."

Don't go into a meeting expecting to come away with a decision or an agreement. Any person who has ever attempted to establish relationships with the Japanese will attest to the fact that there is no such thing as the "Bam, bam, thank you, Ma'am" way of doing business. Rather, patience is a virtue that must be learned if you ever expect a contract to be signed. It may take three visits and a few years for a business relationship to officially get off the ground. By being aware of this before going to Japan, foreigners (or *gaijin*, as the Japanese refer to us) will have a much more realistic attitude about what to expect.

Punctuality

The Japanese operate in a most precise manner. For that reason, it is crucial to be on time for business engagements. Tokyo traffic can be very congested, so allow extra time for travel.

Senior Japanese businesspersons may arrive a few minutes late as a reflection of the demands of their high rank.

Seating Etiquette

Seating etiquette dictates that the highest-level person hosting a meal sits at the center of the table. The most important guest will be seated to the host's immediate right. The least important guest will be seated near the entrance or door.

When sitting down, be sure to place both of your feet on the floor, rather than having the soles of your shoes showing or crossing your legs.

Shoe Etiquette

Whether you are invited to the home of a Japanese person or to a restaurant, or you are staying at a Japanese inn (a *ryokan*), you will be taking off your shoes more in one day than you do in a week in your own country. For that reason, prepare to take socks or stockings that are clean and conservative, and avoid anything that is worn or dirty.

There will be many signs that you should remove your shoes. You may see shoes lined up at the entrance (pointing toward the door). You may also see people approaching you who are wearing slippers rather than shoes. If you are offered a pair of slippers, be sure to put them on to replace your shoes.

As you follow others into a room, be sure to step over the threshold. Also, notice if others remove their slippers when they enter a room with rice mats, known as *tatamis*. If they do, follow suit. Once you are in a room with rice mats on the floor, be sure to avoid walking on the outside border of the mats.

Lastly, be careful to notice if any slippers are placed in front of a bathroom door. Most times, a red pair of slippers in this location means that you should put them on and wear them while you are in the bathroom. One size will fit all. Be sure to remove them upon leaving the bathroom and replace them with the ones you were offered upon your arrival. If slippers were not made available upon your arrival, remain in your socks.

Tea Etiquette

Believe it or not, there is even a set of rituals for accepting a cup of tea and drinking the tea. It begins with a bow as you receive the cup with your right hand. This ritual continues as you balance the cup in the palm of your right hand.

Before you actually drink the tea, turn the cup clockwise three times using your right hand.

Wait for the host to take the first sip. Then, after sipping your tea, it is appropriate to wipe the part of the cup where your lips touched, once again using your right hand.

Before giving your cup back to your host, turn it counterclockwise.

Tipping Tips

As is the case in many other Asian countries, tipping is as uncommon as it is common in the Western world. This means you should not tip cab drivers, hotel bellhops, restaurant servers, etc. (Note: An automatic service charge is built into most restaurant bills.)

If you stay in a *ryokan* and decide to tip your maid, 5 percent of your bill is acceptable.

Toasting Etiquette

If you would like to propose a toast, the appropriate term is *Kampia*, which is the equivalent of "Cheers." After this toast, those around you will repeat your toast and clink and clank glasses before enjoying sake, whiskey, or beer.

Always wait for a toast to be made and the person hosting the meal to take the first sip before you drink your own beverage.

If a toast is proposed to you, be sure to reciprocate with a toast of your own.

When You Are Invited to a Japanese Home

Invitations to a Japanese home are unusual. If you receive such an invitation, you should feel greatly honored.

Remove your coat and shoes before entering the house. Most hosts will provide you with house slippers.

Do not sit until you are invited to do so. When you first sit down, place your legs under you as though you are kneeling. Your host will soon invite you to relax. Men may sit with their legs crossed while women may sit with their legs to either side of them.

Women in Business

Although women are now in higher-ranking positions in Japan than in yesteryear, the majority of them are still on the lower rungs of the ladder in comparison with Western women.

Women should not be surprised if they are not treated with the same respect that they would receive in Western countries or in Europe. For instance, women are not necessarily given the seat of honor under any circumstances. They should also not be expected to be served first, as they would in other parts of the world.

Whatever You Do...

- Don't treat another person's business card with disrespect.
- Don't worry about filling every minute by talking, rather than allowing time for silence.
- Don't be concerned if your Japanese contact waits 10 to 15 seconds before responding.
- Don't think your Japanese contact is sleeping when his or her eyes are closed; this simply means the person may be trying to listen very carefully to what is being said.
- Don't eat every piece of rice in your rice bowl unless you would like your bowl to be replenished.
- Don't take a sip of tea until another person has done so.
- Don't motion for someone to come near you by having your palms facing out; keep them down as you wave your fingers toward you.

- Don't present a gift that has any association with the number 4.

- Don't expect fast decisions or agreements in your business dealings with the Japanese.

- Don't touch another person on the back.

Advice From the Experts

"I would recommend wearing loafers or easy-to-remove shoes. Many homes and most tourist sites (i.e., shrines and temples) request that shoes be left at the door. Obviously, socks should also be in good condition."

—*Douglas E. Darrow, International Operations Quality Leader, General Electric Aircraft Engine Services*

"Never pour your own drink, and keep an eye on your neighbors' beverages during dinner or lunch. Refill their glasses if they are getting low. Also, when someone pours a drink for you, pick up your glass and tip it toward the person replenishing your beverage."

—*Sheila Spradlin, Vice President, Fifth Third Bank*

Chapter 6

Malaysia

---

7 reasons people do business in Malaysia

1. Malaysia's main industries include rubber goods, logging, and electronics.

2. Malaysia has an abundance of natural resources—including oil, bauxite, and iron—which have been instrumental in the country's prosperity.

3. It is one of the world's top producers of tin.

4. The country is a key trading center in the Far East.

5. Most Malaysians engaged in business transactions are fluent in English.

6. Malaysia is the world's leading producer of palm oil.

7. The country is abundant in rice and pepper.

Malaysia is a country separated into two areas on the South China Sea, approximately 600 miles apart. Peninsular Malaysia is located on the southern portion of the Malay Peninsula, just south of Thailand and north of Singapore, and contains 11 states. East Malaysia is located on the northern portion of Borneo Island, and contains two states. Between the two regions, Malaysia covers 127,320 square miles of land. Peninsular Malaysia has numerous mountain ranges, while East Malaysia is largely lowlands, with some high mountains deep inside the country. Dense jungle also marks much of the Malay landscape in both regions.

Malaysia's major industries are tin and oil, although manufacturing has been on the rise. The country also mines and exports minerals such as iron ore, copper, silver, and gold. Chief among the buyers of Malaysia's products are the United States, Great Britain, Germany, Japan, Taiwan, and Singapore.

Malaysia's bicameral parliament is headed by the prime minister, who is the leader of the majority party in the house of representatives. The head of state, known as the *yang di-pertuan agong*, is one of the nine hereditary rulers of the Malay states and is selected by that group to serve a five-year term. Each of the 13 states also has its own unicameral legislature with a chief minister and a titular ruler.

Malaysia was once controlled by the Portuguese and then the Dutch, until Great Britain expanded into the area in the late 1700s and eventually used "advisors" to dictate policy in the Malay region. Certain areas, such as North Borneo and Sarawak, became British protectorates. In 1942, Japan invaded and occupied Malaya,

Sarawak, and North Borneo until the end of World War II. After the war, ethnic and political rivalries, as well as a community-led rebellion, created a period of dissension and strife that threatened the country's inevitable independence from the British Empire. This independence was finally won in the mid-1950s, whereupon Britain helped the country's new rulers work out a new federal constitution. Since then, Malaysian politics have been marred by ethnic disputes and political conflicts. Since 1981, the government has been led by Mahathir bin Muhammad, whose coalition has gained in strength over the years and retained its hold on power in successive elections. Malaysia enjoyed an economic boom in the 1990s that led to the construction of several large projects, including a new federal capital, a new international airport, and a controversial hydroelectric dam. However, several of these large projects were dropped when Malaysian currency went into a decline on the international exchange in 1997.

Statistics and Information

Air Travel

When you arrive in Kuala Lumpur, you will land at the Subang International Airport. If you take a taxi to the hotel where you'll be staying, expect it to take about three-quarters of an hour and to cost US$10-15.

A departure tax is assessed when you leave the country. Here is the tax, according to destination:

- Australia: MYR40 (US$11)
- China: CNY90 (US$10.80)
- Hong Kong: HKD50 (US$6.50)
- Indonesia: IDR21,000 (US$9.40)
- Japan: JPY2,000-2,600 (US$23-29)
- New Zealand: NZD20 (US$11.20)
- The Philippines: PHP500 (US$9.65)
- Singapore: $SGD10 (US$7.10-10.70)

- Taiwan: TOP15 (US$11.20)
- Thailand: THB200 (US$8)
- Vietnam: $20 (the same in US$)

Country Code

The country code for Malaysia is 60.

Major city codes are:

- 05 for Ipoh and Taiping.
- 07 for Johor Baharu.
- 09 for Kota Baharu, Kuala Terengganu, and Kuantan.
- 03 for Kuala Lumpur.
- 082 for Kuching.
- 06 for Malacca and Seremban.
- 04 for Pinang and Sungai Petani.

Currency

Malaysian currency is the *ringgit* or M$. This currency is available in six different denominations: M$1, M$5, M$10, M$50, M$100, and the M$1,000. A *ringgit* is made up of 100 *sen* or cents.

Be sure to make banks your first choice when exchanging money. If visiting a bank is not convenient, look for a money-changer. Your last choice for exchanging money should be hotels, because they give the worst rates.

When exchanging traveler's checks for this country's currency, be sure to have your passport—you'll need it for proper identification.

Dates

Write dates in the following format: day, month, year. January 30, 1999, would be written as 30/1/99.

Ethnic Makeup

Malaysia is a multi-ethnic country, with the majority of the population being Malays. Approximately one third is Chinese and the remainder is a combination of individuals whose roots are from India, Pakistan, and Bangladesh.

Holidays

The following are the holidays that are celebrated throughout the country. Because these are considered national holidays, it is wise to avoid scheduling meetings during these times.

January 1	New Year's Day
January/ February	Chinese New Year
February 1	City Day (Kuala Lumpur)
February/ March	Ramadan
March, May, or June	Hari Raya (Feast of the Sacrifice; based on the lunar calendar)
May 1	Labor Day
May 6	Wesak Day (celebration of the full moon of the Buddha)
June 5	King's Birthday
June 21	Awal Muharram (Islamic New Year)
August 31	National Day
August/ September	The Prophet Mohammed's Birthday
Beginning of November	Deepavali (celebrates the triumph of Krishna over the demon king, Nasakasura; celebrated according to the lunar calendar)
December 25	Christmas Day

Language

Although Bahasa Malay is the official language of Malaysia, Malay is the most widely spoken language. The Chinese who live in Malaysia speak Mandarin. While many dialects are spoken among the Indians living in Malaysia, Tamil and Hindi are the most common languages.

Religion

Several faiths are practiced in Malaysia. More than half of the population practices the Muslim religion, while nearly a fifth follows Buddhism. More than 10 percent of the population observes various religions, while less than 10 percent of the population practices Hindu. Less than 10 percent of the population practices Christianity.

Time Zone Differences

Malaysia is eight hours ahead of Greenwich Mean Time and 13 hours ahead of U.S. Eastern Standard Time.

Weather

Plan for rain! Malaysia usually has a lot of precipitation throughout the year. The monsoon season lasts from September through December. However, even the "off" season sees rain almost daily. Humidity is usually high throughout the year, except in the highlands. Temperatures remain tropical, ranging from 70 to 85 degrees Fahrenheit.

Etiquette

Business Attire

Because Malaysia is very hot all year long, cotton and linen clothes are recommended. Keep the humid climate in mind by packing fabrics that are lightweight.

Conservative attire is appropriate in business situations, especially when first establishing rapport with a new person. Western-style suits should be worn for all business meetings. Men should wear conservative suits consisting of a jacket and tie. Women should wear a suit or conservative business dress with sleeves rather than slacks, which may be considered too informal.

Avoid wearing yellow, because it is the color reserved for Malaysian royalty.

Business Entertaining/Dining

Business entertaining is a must and also a test; the Malays will be watching you to see if you are willing to put effort into establishing a personal relationship with them. Doing so will help to cement successful business relationships.

The development of a business relationship often centers on food. Therefore, it is good manners to accept a little of whatever is offered, rather than refuse it.

The left hand is considered taboo; it should not be used for eating or handling food in any way or form.

If you are hosting a meal, remember that your Muslim guests should not be offered either pork or alcohol. Similarly, Hindus and Sikhs should not be served beef, because cows are considered sacred in those religions.

Malaysia is composed of a number of different ethnic groups, so utensil etiquette varies. For instance, individuals of Malaysian and Indian descent may choose to use the fork as the scooper (using the left hand) and the spoon as the utensil that takes the food to the mouth (using the right hand). Some individuals may even use their hands (the right one only) to take food to their mouths. Your best bet is to follow the person with whom you are dining.

If you are dining with an individual of Chinese descent, that person will probably use chopsticks as the eating utensil, while a spoon may also be used for soup. Once again, you should follow suit.

When you invite Malays to dinner, you may choose to include spouses, but do not plan on talking business if they attend.

While it is not considered appropriate to hail a cab by raising your hand in mid-air, it is the correct gesture for getting the attention of a server in a restaurant.

Whoever initiates the invitation picks up the check.

Conversation

Most Malaysians are proud of their heritage and their families. Malaysians also enjoy sports, especially soccer. Inquiring about any of these topics is a great way to get the ball rolling and to show your sincere interest.

Questions that individuals from other cultures might consider ill-mannered or too personal are often acceptable in the Malaysian culture—for instance, whether you are married or single, the amount of money you make, and so on. When you are asked such questions, you may choose to be vague or even change the subject rather than answer them.

Overt questions about religion or customs may be interpreted as criticism. Avoid openly criticizing or implying criticism of anyone or anything about the culture. Do not bring up politics or religion.

Gestures and Public Manners

Etiquette dictates that shoes and hats be removed before entering a mosque or temple. It is also considered good form to step over the threshold rather than on it.

When going to a mosque or temple, dress conservatively. For women, dress should include long pants and/or skirts around the knees or longer, as well as tops with sleeves; sleeveless tops should definitely not be worn. Women should also have their heads covered. If other people put on a garment similar to a robe before entering, follow suit.

When pointing at a person or object, the appropriate way to do so is by extending your right hand with your thumb extended and fingers folded under.

As in other Asian countries, a smile has many different meanings (happiness, annoyance, shyness, embarrassment, and so on). Keep this in mind when someone smiles at you.

Malaysians believe a person's soul resides in the head, so never touch anyone on the head, not even a child.

When passing an object, reaching for something, or touching someone (such as shaking hands), do so with your right hand. The left hand is considered unclean and should not be used in contact with others, to eat, or to pass things.

Do not move objects around with your feet at any time; use your hands only.

When sitting, be sure your shoes are facing the ground rather than showing the soles, which is considered rude.

The only acceptable contact between sexes is a handshake. Holding hands and walking arm in arm is normal between people of the same sex and should merely be interpreted as a sign of friendship.

When exiting a room, say "excuse me," and add a slight bow.

Do not pound your fist into the palm of your other hand, because this is considered an obscene gesture.

When hailing a taxi, salute to get a driver's attention, rather than waving your hand in the air.

Gift-giving Etiquette

Gifts should not be exchanged at first meetings. Only after you have established a personal relationship with an associate should you present him or her with a gift.

Be sure to go to Malaysia prepared with gifts. They will come in handy when you are yourself presented a gift in a business situation or are invited to someone's home.

Recommended business gifts include any item that is representative of your city or country, quality office accessories, pens, etc.

Recommended social gifts include something representative of your home country or a food that may be considered a delicacy.

Be sure to know a person's religious practices in order to know what gifts may be inappropriate. For example, Muslims should not be given pork, alcohol, or anything that has to do with dogs.

Those of Indian descent will appreciate receiving gifts in odd numbers, such as 1, 11, 21, and so on, because this is considered lucky. Avoid giving gifts in multiples of three, because this number is considered bad luck.

When giving a gift to someone of Chinese descent, avoid anything that may be misinterpreted as an indication of your wanting to sever ties (scissors or knives, for example) or that is associated with death (a clock, white flowers, etc.).

Do not wrap your gift with white paper, because this color is associated with death and mourning rituals. Blue, black, and yellow gift wrap should also be avoided.

Give and receive gifts with both hands and set them aside to open once the giver has gone. Don't open your gift in his or her presence.

Be sure not to give a gift so costly that the recipient will feel obligated to you. Keep it simple and inexpensive. In this regard, when receiving a gift, take care not to reciprocate with one of greater value compared to the present you received.

Greetings and Introductions

When greeting a Malaysian during the morning hours, the term to use is *Salamat pagi*. During afternoon hours, the proper term is, *Salamat petant*.

When introducing a man and a woman, the female's name should be said first.

Just as in most other countries, when presenting a higher-ranking person to a more junior person, the more senior person's name is said first.

When you are being introduced to a Malaysian woman, be sure to shake hands with her only if she has extended her hand. If she does not extend her hand, a smile and a nod will be the gesture you should use to greet her.

It is very important to show respect for elders, even on a personal level.

Malays should be addressed by their first names preceded by the equivalent of "Mr." (*Encik*), "Mrs." (*Puan*), or "Miss" (*Cik*). On the other hand, Muslims use only a first name followed by *bin* (son of) or *binti* (daughter of), plus their father's first name. Chinese and Indians may be greeted with their last name preceded by Mr., Mrs., or Ms. Keep in mind that the Chinese place their last name before their first and should be addressed accordingly.

As is the case in several other Asian countries, the exchange of business cards is an important part of meeting and greeting rituals. Thus, be sure to take plenty of cards with you.

When meeting a Malay, you may be extended a hand for shaking; however, the person may choose instead to greet you with a cultural Malay greeting called a *namaste*. This involves touching both palms at heart level as a slight bow is made.

When meeting a Muslim, be sure to shake hands. If this person wants to show you that he is very pleased to meet you, he may put his right hand on his heart after shaking hands. You may choose to reciprocate by also putting your right hand on your heart after shaking hands.

Always refer to individuals in Parliament as "Your Honorable."

The highest respect should always be shown to royalty. If you know you are going to meet a member of royalty, be sure to go prepared with a gift (see Gift-giving Etiquette). Stand with your hands at your sides, unless you are greeting the royal, in which case you must bow with your palms pressed together before you at chest level. Allow any member of royalty to depart a room before you do.

Meeting Manners

In Malaysia, believing in the other person is vital to a strong business relationship. One way to get to know each other is through small talk, which is an important part of establishing rapport. Use this conversation as a way to get to know the other person, and also to allow this individual to become acquainted with you.

Negotiations will be lengthy and you should have every detail of your proposal worked out before presenting it.

Just as in developing business relationships with the Japanese, building long-term relationships with individuals from Malaysia is a long-term process. Therefore, expect to travel to Malaysia a few times before the decision-making process is solidified. Even once you have reached a decision with your Malaysian associates, they may try to renegotiate. Written contracts aren't regarded as set in stone.

Punctuality

Although punctuality is not a priority for Malays, you should nevertheless make a point of being on time for appointments. Even if you know you are going to be kept waiting, you should still arrive on time.

Seating Etiquette

Seating should be dictated by the host or the highest Malaysian officer in attendance.

Seating will most likely follow the common Asian practice of hierarchical order. Just as in the United States, the host should be seated to the immediate left of the most senior guest. This guest should be given the best seat at the table, which is usually the farthest from the door.

Tipping Tips

Tipping is not the custom in Malaysia, because service charges are included in most services. Restaurants add a 4-percent service charge, but you can leave more money if you received good service.

While tipping a taxi driver is not necessary, when paying the driver, it is appropriate to request that the person keep any odd change in coins.

It is both acceptable and expected for you to tip porters. The appropriate amount is one *ringgit* per piece of luggage. You may also tip individuals who provide hotel room service for you (50 *sen*).

When You Are Invited to a Malay Home

An invitation by a Malaysian to his or her home should be considered quite a compliment. Arrive anywhere up to a half-hour *after* the originally stated time. Guests should take gifts to be presented to the hostess. A box of chocolates or fruits is acceptable.

The meal may be buffet style. Wait until your host gives you a cue before serving yourself. Men and women may eat separately.

Plan on staying and socializing for about an hour after the meal.

If you are in the home of a Muslim, you may be seated on the floor. It is considered correct for men to sit with their legs crossed while women may sit with their legs either beneath their feet or tucked under their left sides.

Women in Business

Western women will encounter few problems conducting business in Malaysia.

Feel free to invite male colleagues to socialize. Include spouses if you'd like.

Women traveling alone should take extra precautions by dining in hotel restaurants.

Whatever You Do...

- Don't serve pork or alcohol to your Muslim guest, or give alcohol as a gift to a Muslim.
- Don't point at a person or object by extending your forefinger.
- Don't use your left hand for taking food to your mouth when eating with your Indian or Muslim guests.
- Don't put your hands in your pockets. It is considered impolite.
- Don't allow your dog to have free reign of the house when entertaining Muslims.
- Don't "scoot" objects with your feet; use only your hands to move things.

• Don't hail a cab by raising your hand in midair, as this is considered inappropriate. Instead, use a salute to attract a driver.

Advice From the Experts

"Most of the country is Muslim. My experience is that meetings should be scheduled around prayer times. Prayer rooms are strictly off limits to non-Muslims. Friday around noon is a very busy prayer time. In fact, many companies close the office on Friday afternoons."

—*Douglas E. Darrow, International Operations Quality Leader, General Electric Aircraft Engine Services*

Chapter 7

New Zealand

8 reasons people do business in New Zealand

1. New Zealand has an abundance of natural resources, including gas, iron, coal, and gold.

2. Other important resources are wool and timber.

3. Industries that contribute to New Zealand's strong economic growth include food processing, textiles, machinery, fishing, and forest products.

4. New Zealand does more than one billion dollars in tourism business annually.

5. This country provides easy access to Australia and other countries in the Far East and Pacific Rim.

6. New Zealand's customs and manners are similar to the Western Hemisphere's and English is the first language there.

7. New Zealand is a country free of major pollutants.

8. The people of New Zealand are hard-working, and yet can be informal in their behavior.

New Zealand is a long and narrow country located in the South Pacific Ocean, southeast of Australia. It consists of two large islands (North Island and South Island) and one smaller island (Stewart Island), along with a number of even smaller islands. The land is largely mountainous, but is also marked by rain forests, deserts, swamps, plains, and volcanoes. It is also noteworthy for many magnificent rivers and lakes, such as Waikaremoana and Wanaka.

Wellington is the capital of New Zealand. More than 70 percent of the population of 3.7 million people live on North Island. Of these, more than 1 million people live in or around Auckland. The country's economy is largely agricultural, with its biggest exports being dairy, meat, and wool. The government is a constitutional monarchy, with power resting in the parliament, headed by the prime minister, who is the leader of the majority party. The monarch's duties are largely ceremonial and advisory in nature. A new parliament is elected every three years.

New Zealand was originally populated by Polynesians, until the 1600s, when Europeans such as Dutch explorer Abel Tasman began landing on its shores, followed by British Captain James Cook in 1769. Although originally repulsed by the native Maoris, the British soon began to colonize the land, which was regarded in the beginning as an extension of the Australian continent. For some time, tensions between the settlers (called "Pakeha") and the Maoris escalated until a war broke out in the 1860s, resulting in the Maoris' defeat. Gold mining and sheep farming eventually brought prosperity to the country. New

Zealand was granted autonomy from Great Britain in 1931 and independence in 1947. Since then, the Maori population and culture has been on the rise, and in recent years discord has once again been experienced between Pakeha and Maori.

Statistics and Information

Air Travel

There are three international airports serving New Zealand. They are located in Auckland, Wellington, and Christchurch. Auckland's airport is the one most commonly used by international travelers.

Upon arrival, prepare to display proof that you have a return flight that has already been paid. Also expect to pay a $20 departure tax when leaving New Zealand.

Country Code

New Zealand's country code is 64.

Major city codes include:

• 9 for Auckland.

• 3 for Christchurch.

• 4 for Wellington.

Currency

The country's currency is the New Zealand dollar (NZ$). Coins are in 5-, 10-, 20-, and 50-cent pieces, as well as $1 and $2. Bills come in denominations of NZ$5, $10, $20, $50, and $100.

When exchanging traveler's checks, a bank will have the best exchange rate. Be sure to have your passport, because you will need it for proper identification. While hotels may be more convenient, you will pay a higher fee.

Dates

To write a date, place the day before the month, followed by the year. For example, March 15, 1999, would be written 15 March 1999, or 15/3/99.

Ethnic Makeup

Europeans of various backgrounds, predominantly British, account for about 90 percent of New Zealand's population. Approximately 2 percent of the individuals in New Zealand are of Pacific Island descent.

Native New Zealanders are called Maoris. They are trying hard to preserve their culture, but because they comprise less than 10 percent of the country's population, this is becoming increasingly difficult.

Holidays

The following are the holidays celebrated throughout and/or in specific areas of New Zealand. It is wise to avoid scheduling meetings during these times.

January 1	New Year's Day
February 6	Waitargi Day (a celebration of the signing of the peace treaty between the Maoris and the Caucasian settlers)
Friday in early April	Good Friday
Sunday following Good Friday	Easter
April 25	Anzac Day (a celebration to memorialize the Australian and New Zealand Army Corps)
June 8	Queen's Birthday
October 26	Labour Day
December 25	Christmas Day
December 26	Boxing Day

Language

The country's official language is English. However, don't be surprised if you have a difficult time understanding a New Zealander. Heavy accents and different terms for familiar items may make communication more challenging than you would expect.

Maori is also spoken.

Religion

Although less than 20 percent of the population claims to practice no religion, British influence exists. For that reason, Christianity is the largest religion practiced by more than approximately 25 percent of New Zealanders, with Anglicanism, Presbyterianism, and Catholicism being the largest denominations.

Time Zone Differences

New Zealand is ahead of Greenwich Mean Time by 12 hours and ahead of United States Eastern Standard Time by 17 hours.

Daylight Savings begins the first Sunday in October and runs through the last Sunday in March.

Weather

Although the temperature generally stays mild throughout the year, the only sure bet with New Zealand's weather is that it is always changing.

Like Australia, seasons in New Zealand are the reverse of those in the Western world. When the United States is experiencing summer, this country is in its winter season, and vice versa.

New Zealand's winter is also its rainy season, so be sure to carry an umbrella during that time. Winter temperatures throughout the country are usually around the low 60s and summer temperatures are around the low 70s.

Etiquette

Business Attire

Westerners should wear the same professional attire in New Zealand that they wear for meetings in their own country. Sport coats and trousers may be considered too informal, so men should wear business suits.

When packing for your trip to New Zealand, be sure to remember that the seasons are the opposite of those in Western countries. Thus, heavier clothing should be taken when traveling to New Zealand during the summer months and lighter-weight clothing should be packed during the winter months.

Business Entertaining/Dining

Business is usually conducted in social settings, such as during meals, sporting events, and cultural activities. When you initiate a meeting, suggest lunch or dinner. New Zealanders also enjoy a trip to the horse races or a rugby match. Spouses and children may be included in your invitation.

"Morning tea" is a very common practice around 10-10:30 a.m. "Afternoon tea" is also common. In both cases, tea and scones or another light pastry will be served. When you are invited simply to "tea," you should recognize that this term refers to "dinner," which takes place anytime after 6 p.m.

Follow correct European dining style. Be sure to allow your host to set the pace for the meal.

Few New Zealand restaurants have liquor licenses; however, they do allow you to bring your own alcoholic beverages. Check a restaurant's policy before you invite associates to dine.

What Westerners call an "entree" is the equivalent of an appetizer in New Zealand. To inquire about an entree, refer to it as a "main."

A meal of roast hogget (baby lamb), topped with mint sauce and gravy, potatoes, parsnips, and pumpkin is often a family favorite.

Fresh fruit and salads of all sorts are usually served with each meal or alone as a meal. New Zealand is also known for its excellent seafood.

Finally, when you are hosting a meal, ask for the "bill" rather than the "check."

Conversation

New Zealanders—who are also called "Kiwis"— are lively people who enjoy conversing with new friends. They will not hesitate to begin a conversation with a stranger, whether they are waiting for a bus, are in line at a public location, or just about anywhere.

Many Kiwis are active people who engage in outdoor activities, such as sailing, biking, and rugby, which is their national pastime. Thus, sports and anything to do with the outdoors are favorite topics for discussion.

Kiwis love to be consulted for help or advice, so feel free to ask.

Topics to avoid: Stay away from national politics, religion, and racial issues.

Gestures and Public Manners

New Zealanders are solemn, "get it done" people. Displays of emotion in public are frowned upon, because they may draw unwanted attention. Equal treatment and personal responsibility are of great importance in the Kiwi culture.

Kiwis don't relish formality, therefore being casual is acceptable, as long as you are polite. Common courtesy is expected and is often carried to extensive lengths—for instance, giving your seat up on the bus, apologizing profusely for inconveniencing or hurting somebody else, and treating others as you would like to be treated.

It is considered impolite to use a toothpick or to chew gum in front of others.

When making the peace or victory sign, be sure to extend your index finger and middle finger straight up, with your palm away from you. If you turn your palm inward or toward you, it will be interpreted as a very crude gesture.

Gift-giving Etiquette

Gift-giving is not the ceremonious event in New Zealand that it is in Asian countries. It is done out of common courtesy rather than "pomp and circumstance."

A small token of appreciation is appropriate when attending a business meeting, social function, or a meal at someone's home. Keep the gift simple, because Kiwis dislike showy gestures. Flowers, wine, or chocolate are fine.

Greetings and Introductions

During an initial meeting, New Zealanders may appear rigid and unfriendly. Don't let this first impression make you feel unwelcome. New Zealanders are undemonstrative people by nature. For that reason, they may appear more formal and restrained until rapport has been established with others.

When greeting a New Zealander, begin with a "How do you do." The term, "Hello" should be reserved for subsequent meetings. Also, Western-style handshakes should be exchanged. Women should extend their hands to men, because men from New Zealand seldom initiate this contact.

Titles such as "Mr.," Mrs.," and Dr." should be used when greeting a New Zealander. First names may be used only after you are invited to do so.

The term "G'day" is the most common exchange between friends.

The business card exchange is more a convenience than a formality. Unlike Asians, who make a ceremony out of presenting cards, Kiwis are too laid back for that. However, it will be important for you to have plenty of cards on hand to exchange with business contacts. Your business cards will assist others in remembering your name and also provide necessary information on how you can be reached.

Meeting Manners

Arrive on time and be ready to make a well-informed presentation. Have neat, precise literature providing some background on your company and outlining your proposal. Do not go to great lengths to make your handouts showy or fancy, because New Zealanders prefer to avoid flamboyant displays.

Although Kiwis are relaxed in their business affairs, they move more quickly than their Australian neighbors. Therefore, use your judgment to gauge the pace at which you should proceed.

New Zealanders make decisions based on facts and experience rather than personal feelings. Still, the effect a decision will have on others is of primary concern.

Punctuality

New Zealanders place great value on punctuality. Therefore, it is in order to be on time or early when attending business or social engagements.

Seating Etiquette

There are no rigid rules governing seating. Allow your host or the most senior member of the Kiwi team to suggest the seating arrangement.

Tipping Tips

New Zealand attaches a 12.5-percent Goods and Service Tax (GST) on most services, so tipping is rare. The only exception should be for outstanding service, at which time a tip of 5 to 10 percent would be appropriate.

When You Are Invited to a New Zealand Home

Because New Zealanders love to entertain, you will most likely be invited to their homes. You may even be asked to join your associate's family for a meal.

"Tea" is the term for the large meal (dinner) of the day and is served as late as 8 p.m.

Women in Business

Women make up 44 percent of New Zealand's work force. For this reason, Western businesswomen will encounter very little difference in the way business is conducted in this country.

Women doing business in New Zealand should take the initiative of extending their hand for handshakes. This will alleviate any moments of hesitation that Kiwi men may experience when establishing a professional rapport with women.

Whatever You Do...

- Don't mistake a New Zealander for an Australian. There is much rivalry between these countries and this could be considered an insult.

- Don't speak in a loud voice. It will annoy most New Zealanders.

- Don't ask where the "bathroom" is, unless you plan on taking a bath. When you merely want to use the facilities, ask to be shown to the toilet or the "loo."

- Don't forget that the seasons are reversed in the Southern Hemisphere. Many New Zealanders will be on summer vacation when people on other continents are experiencing winter.

- Don't expect vegetarian meals to be readily available if you are a strict vegetarian. New Zealand is much more of a "meat and potatoes" culture. If you are willing to eat fish or chicken instead, you will be fine.

- Don't expect to understand the language in New Zealand, even though it will be English. Many expressions vary.

- Don't be surprised if a Kiwi prolongs eye contact with you; this is considered appropriate.

- Don't consider it rude if your New Zealand client brings up the subject of U.S. politics. You will find the Kiwis to be well-versed in this topic.

- Don't be surprised if a New Zealander goes out of his or her way to give you directions, suggest a restaurant, and so on. Most Kiwis take pride in giving recommendations about their country.

- Don't misunderstand the term "roll up" for anything except "to close." Most banks, shops, and offices "roll up" at 5 p.m.

Chapter 8

The Philippines

---

7 reasons people do business in the Philippines

1. It is a country highly advanced in business systems and procedures.
2. This country is rich in minerals and energy resources.
3. The Philippines produces the most copper in all of Asia.
4. The Philippines' agricultural resources include sugar, coconut, and grains.
5. Another important industry in the Philippines is food processing.
6. The export business is booming, especially in the computer field and advertising.
7. The Philippines is known for its textiles, wood products, and pharmaceuticals.

The Philippine Islands are located in the western Pacific Ocean, at the north end of Malay Archipelago, between Taiwan and Borneo. The country is bounded by the Philippine Sea on the east, the South China Sea on the west, and the Celebes Sea on the south. Within this area there are approximately 7,100 islands, only 11 of which are larger than 1,000 square miles, supporting the majority of the population. All the islands consist primarily of a partly submerged chain of volcanic mountains. There are some 20 active volcanoes, and earthquakes are quite common throughout the islands.

Luzon is the largest island, followed by Mindanao. Other islands include Samar, Negros, Palawan, Panay, Mindoro, Leyte, Cebu, Bohol, and Masbate. Altogether, the Philippines cover approximately 115,830 square miles of land. Principal assets of the land are rich forest and mineral resources, including gold, silver, copper, iron, slate, cola, limestone, and petroleum, among other minerals.

The majority of the Filipino population is of Malay descent and is divided into groups according to their language and religion. Principal of these are the Tagalogs, the Visayans, and the Ilokanos. The name "Filipino" refers to these Christian Malayan peoples, although it originally meant a person of Spanish descent born in the Philippines. The country's non-Malay inhabitants include Spanish and Chinese descendants, as well as two Muslim groups, the Moro and the Samal. This mixture of groups, languages, and traditions, as well as influences imported from the West, has resulted in no single cultural identity for the natives of the Philippines.

Once under Spanish control, the archipelago was given to the United States to govern in 1898. Nine years later, a government with a bicameral legislature was established, although the country remained under U.S. control until 1935, when independence was granted and a new commonwealth was established with the provision that the United States continue to maintain military bases on the islands. The new government was provisional and submitted to U.S. supervision until 1946, at which time, the country became fully autonomous as the Republic of the Philippines. Nevertheless, U.S. influence remained strong, and military bases remained. Over the years, the government contended with rebellion and dissension, and in 1972 President Ferdinand Marcos declared martial law, which ended in 1981. His successor as president, Corazon Aquino, put through a new constitution in 1987. The country continues to experience internal dissension, although it has become more stabilized in recent years.

Statistics and Information

Air and Land Travel

When you land at the Manila airport, you will have several options for transportation. While limousines are the most dependable, they are also the most costly. Even though taxis are not allowed in the area where you will arrive, you will be able to catch one by going to the departure level of the airport.

Be sure you find out how much you are going to be charged before getting into a cab, otherwise you run the risk of being overcharged. Also be prepared to pay more for air-conditioned cabs.

Country Code

The Philippines' country code is 63.

The major city codes are:

- 32 for Cebu.
- 35 for Davao.
- 2 for Manila.

When you are in the Philippines and would like to make an international call, dial 001.

A Philippine telephone number can consist of either six or seven digits.

Currency

1 *peso* (P) is equivalent to 100 *centavos*.

Unlike other Asian countries, when you are in the Philippines, you actually have a choice of places where you can receive comparable exchange rates. Thus, you can base your decision of where to exchange money on convenience rather than rate.

When exchanging traveler's checks for this country's currency, be sure to have your passport—you will need it for identification.

Dates

Dates are written listing the month, day, and then year. In other words, April 5, 1999, would be written 4/5/99.

Ethnic Makeup

More than 90 percent of the people of the Philippines are of Christian Malay descent. Less than 5 percent are Malay Muslims, with just under 2 percent being Chinese. The remaining 3 percent are a combination of minorities.

Holidays

The following are national holidays celebrated throughout the country. Because these are considered national holidays, it is wise to avoid scheduling meetings during these times.

January 1	New Year's Day
Thursday before Easter	Maundy Thursday
April *	Good Friday
April *	Easter

April 9	Bataan (also called Heroism Day)
May 1	Labor Day
June 12	Independence Day
Last Sunday in August	National Heroes Day
November 1	All Saint's Day
November 30	Bonifacio Day (a celebration of Filipino heroes, especially Andres Bonifacio, who headed the revolutionary movement against the Spanish)
December 25	Christmas Day
December 30	Rizal Day (a day honoring Dr. Jose Rizal, a national hero killed on December 30, 1896)

* These holidays are observed on the first Friday and Sunday following the paschal full moon. For that reason, they change from year to year.

Language

Although most people speak English, the national language of the Philippines is Filipino. This language is based on Tagalog. Business transactions, however, are generally discussed in English.

Religion

Most Filipinos are strict in their religious observances. More than 80 percent practice Roman Catholicism. Approximately 10 percent are Protestants, and 5 percent are Muslims.

Time Zone Differences

The Philippines is eight hours ahead of Greenwich Mean Time and 13 hours ahead of U.S. Eastern Standard Time.

Weather

Tropical climates dominate the mountainous regions of the Philippines. Temperatures range from the 70s to mid-80s Fahrenheit. Manila is usually very warm, with temperatures in the mid-80s in January and as high as the low 90s (Fahrenheit) in June. The country's rainy season lasts from June through November.

Etiquette

Business Attire

Filipinos take much pride in their grooming and beauty, and also form judgments about position, power, and authority based on attire. Thus, you should be fastidious about the way you dress. Your professional presence will also be instrumental in the way you are treated.

Appropriate attire for men includes suits with either open-neck white shirts or shirts with ties. Women will be taken much more seriously when wearing knee-length skirts and conservative necklines; slacks should be avoided. Fashionable and bright-colored suits and dresses are recommended, and should be well-made in good quality fabrics.

Business Entertaining/Dining

Unlike in many other Asian cultures, spouses are included in evening business entertainment. When you are hosting a dinner, be sure to confirm the engagement a day or two in advance, because RSVPs are frequently disregarded by Filipinos.

When you would like to get a server's attention, use your entire hand (palm down) to request the person assist you. Whatever you do, don't try to get the server's attention by raising your index finger and moving it toward you.

Women typically refrain from alcoholic beverages and instead consume fruit juices or soft drinks.

Filipinos take great pride in their cuisine and much of life revolves around food. Because of its rich cultural history, Filipino cuisine combines flavors from South Asia, China, and Spain for a delicious and unique taste.

Filipino dining etiquette follows the Western style. Meals are served family style with the revolving tray in the center of the table. The person hosting the meal will usually order a variety of dishes that will be served at one time. It is considered good manners to wait until the host invites you to begin eating.

The proper utensils to use for eating are a fork and spoon. The fork should remain in the left hand and act as a scooper for placing the food onto the spoon, which should be held in the right hand.

Filipino etiquette dictates that you always leave something on your plate to show that you were satisfied with the portion served to you.

Whoever initiates the invitation picks up the bill.

Conversation

Small talk is an important part of establishing business relationships with Filipinos. Safe topics of conversation include sports, such as basketball, the culture and customs of the Philippines, family, and fiestas.

It is better to avoid any topic that might embarrass a Filipino, as well as politics and religion. For example, don't make any comments about a Filipino having two sets of wives and children. Although this dual marital status is common in the Philippines, it is not discussed. Also, like people from many other countries, Filipinos are very proud. Therefore, never criticize or argue with a Filipino in public.

Gestures and Public Manners

When you are talking with a Filipino, be sure to break eye contact at regular intervals rather than maintaining direct eye contact. If you maintain constant eye contact, the person may perceive you as gawking rather than showing that you are a good listener by giving him or her your full attention with your eyes.

Be sure to maintain harmony and balance with others in public by making only positive comments. Negativity of any sort could cause another to lose face, which could in turn cost you the respect and perhaps even friendship of those around you.

Filipino etiquette dictates that you remain low-keyed in your actions, expressions, and hand gestures, and draw as little attention to yourself as possible.

Being low-keyed also applies to your voice. When talking, make sure that you use an "indoor" rather than an "outdoor" voice. Your tone and volume should remain low rather than loud. A controlled tone will help to project confidence. It may even assist you in being more productive with your Filipino transactions.

When it is necessary to walk between two people, lower your head with your hands clasped in front of you as you pass them. This gesture is a sign of respect.

When motioning for someone to come towards you, place your palm face down moving your fingers towards you.

When pointing towards an object or person, do so with eyes down. Pointing may also be done by puckering your lips and pointing with your mouth.

The appropriate way to indicate the number "two" is by raising your ring finger and pinkie (rather than your index and middle fingers).

Gift-giving Etiquette

Giving gifts to your Filipino contacts is an essential step in building strong business ties and serves as a sign of friendship and respect. Appropriate gifts include something related to your home city, a fine pen, or quality stationery imprinted with your company logo.

Once a contract has been signed, prepare to give your new partners a gift of greater magnitude. These gifts include dinner at a fine restaurant, whiskey for men, and perfume for women. Whatever you do, avoid being so lavish in your gift that it is perceived as bribery.

When you receive a gift, follow the Asian way by not opening it in front of the giver, but wait until you are alone.

Unlike many other Asian countries, there are no restrictions about what colors of wrapping paper to avoid.

Greetings and Introductions

The Filipinos are a very hospitable and compassionate people. Westerners who extend the same warmth will be treated favorably.

Greeting etiquette consists of a light handshake and a smile while looking directly at the person with raised eyebrows. These gestures should be followed by an exchange of business cards.

While men may shake hands with women, they should do so only after the woman has initiated it.

As with Westerners, Filipinos have a given or first name followed by a middle and family or last name. Because formality is key, "Mr.," "Mrs.," or "Miss" should be used unless asked to do otherwise. If someone is introduced with a title (engineer, doctor, lawyer, etc.) that title should be used in place of "Mr.," "Mrs.," or "Miss." If a woman is introduced with two last names, they may be her family name and also her husband's last name. When addressing her, be sure to use both names preceded by either "Mrs." or her title.

When you do not know a person's last name, display respect by using the terms "Sir" or "Ma'am."

As in other Asian countries, the business card exchange is an important part of the relationship development process. For that reason, take plenty of cards with you that emphasize your title, which helps Filipinos to determine your clout and decision-making ability.

When presenting and receiving business cards, do so with both hands. Study the one you receive and comment on it before either laying it on the table in front of you or carefully putting it in your business card case.

How Decisions Are Made

Decision-making is a gradual process made exclusively by senior management. Patience is a virtue that must be practiced when you are in negotiations with Filipinos.

Just as in many other countries, the best way to develop a relationship with a Filipino organization is to arrange for someone to introduce you to a decision-maker within the organization. By making these arrangements, the top people within this company will be more interested in becoming acquainted with your organization than they would if you placed a call to them on your own.

One way that people will spare you from being embarrassed is by saying yes to you when the answer is not really an affirmative one. Instead, the term, "yes" can mean "if you say so," "we'll see," "I understand," or perhaps just plain "no." Thus, take care when you hear the word "yes" and make sure that it really means yes.

When you do not have a clear idea of the decision that has been made, wait a few days and then follow up with your contact. At that time, the person may give you a better idea about where he or she is in the decision-making process.

Meeting Manners

Recognizing key differences in business practices can be the ticket to success when doing business in the Philippines. In addition to maintaining harmony at all costs, humility is an important attribute. For instance, rather than trying to take control by pitching your organization's accomplishments, allow your Filipino counterpart to set the tone of the meeting.

It will be of utmost importance to take note of others' titles and the place in which they are seated, because this is based on hierarchy.

The beginning of the meeting should be reserved for establishing rapport—for instance, by engaging in small talk or by enjoying a meal together prior to the start of the meeting. You may also work on rapport before the meeting takes place by getting together for a sports outing or the like.

When another person is talking, be sure to listen intently without interrupting. Breaking in while someone else is talking is considered offensive.

While humor may not have a place in some meetings, a joke or two is acceptable in a Filipino meeting.

There is a Filipino term called *pakikisma*, which emphasizes the importance of fellowship and making group decisions. This is an important concept to be aware of as you conduct negotiations.

Punctuality and Deadlines

Because promptness is not observed in the same manner as it is in other countries, don't expect meetings or social functions to begin on time. Between heavy traffic and a relaxed attitude about time, it is common for scheduled meetings to be delayed 15 to 20 minutes. Also, deadlines are not viewed with the same finality as they are in the West. Nevertheless, you should make every effort to be prompt yourself, so that you do not keep your Filipino customer waiting.

Seating Etiquette

For both business meetings and entertaining, seating arrangements are based on the hierarchical position of each person in attendance. Your Filipino counterpart should be seated across from you.

Rather than seating yourself when you first arrive, etiquette dictates that you wait for your host to direct you to your seat.

Tipping Tips

Tipping is expected throughout the Philippines. Whether or not a service charge already has been added to a restaurant bill, a small tip should still be left.

If you have received assistance from a hotel concierge, be sure to leave between P20 and P30 for the person.

In addition to the fare, taxi drivers should receive whatever rounded-out amount is closest to the P5 to P10, or 10 percent of the fare.

Doormen and porters should be given between P10 and P20.

When You Are Invited to a Filipino Home

Consider it an honor if you are invited to a Filipino home. This invitation is a true display of camaraderie and shows the high degree of comfort that your host feels with you.

Although it is not expected, it will be appreciated if you take a small gift, such as flowers, wine, or cake for the spouse of the host.

Be sure to arrive 15 to 20 minutes after the time given in the invitation. If you arrive early or on time, you may unknowingly be rushing the host and may even be perceived as overanxious.

Prepare to be asked to remove your shoes or wear the house slippers provided to you.

Many business-class families have cooks to prepare their food, so don't be too lavish in your praise of the meal, as it is not considered good manners to do more than comment on the food. If you would like to pay a compliment, say something positive about the home decor or the flowers—in other words, something that has been arranged by the host or spouse rather than the cook.

Finally, avoid referring to your host's spouse as his "hostess." In the Philippines, this term refers to a prostitute.

Women in Business

Despite the fact that Filipinas still have limited rights in political and legal arenas, they have become an integral part of the business world, where they enjoy more sexual equality than in other Asian countries.

Filipinas in business are expected to be just as productive and competent as their male counterparts. However, the concept of "machismo," or the need for men to prove and exhibit their masculinity, dictates that women not be domineering, but instead behave and dress in a "feminine" manner.

Whatever You Do...

- Don't forget to confirm all engagements a day or two in advance. Because a yes is not necessarily a concrete affirmative response, what you may consider to be a definite appointment may not be the case in the mind of a Filipino.

- Don't anticipate speedy business transactions. Time is viewed in a much-less-structured way in the Philippines.

- Don't be surprised if men have two families. Although it is not socially acknowledged, it is common for a man to have a mistress and children outside of his marriage.
- Don't put your hands on your hips when talking. This gesture can be misconstrued that you are challenging the person.
- Don't be surprised if you hear people hissing in restaurants. This is a common way of getting the attention of servers.
- Don't misinterpret a smile as a gesture of happiness. This nonverbal act can also mean that the person is embarrassed.
- Don't be surprised if someone raises his or her eyebrows at you. It is one way of showing that you have been understood.
- Don't be extremely direct when communicating with Filipinos. The indirect approach will be better received.
- Don't eat everything on your plate. If you do, your Filipino host may misinterpret your hearty appetite as not having served you enough food.

Chapter 9

Singapore

10 reasons people do business in Singapore

1. This Asian country is one of the world's largest ports.

2. Singapore is an international financial center.

3. The government has limited restrictions on foreign ownership.

4. There are no tariff barriers.

5. The Singaporean government is committed to free enterprise.

6. Businesses in Singapore welcome foreign investors.

7. Singaporeans are a well-educated people.

8. Singapore has worked hard to become a strong socioeconomic success through manufacturing.

9. Singapore provides a solid base for high-tech industries.

10. This country is known for its oil refining, electronics, banking, food, rubber processing, and biotechnology.

Welcome to Singapore, the Garden City of Asia. This Pacific-Rim island at the end of the Malay Peninsula lies between the South China Sea and the Indian Ocean. The country includes 58 nearby islands. Singapore has a population of three million, three quarters of whom live on approximately 225 square miles. Besides being one of the wealthiest nations in Asia, Singapore is a very orderly society. The people are, for the most part, descended from immigrants from China, the Malay Peninsula, Sri Lanka, and the Indian subcontinent. This has provided for a rich mix of ethnicities and cultures.

In 1819, the British established a trading post in Singapore, accomplished when Sir Stamford Raffles negotiated a treaty with the rulers of Singapore, Sultan Hussein of Johor, and the Temenggong. The settlement quickly became a trading powerhouse in Southeast Asia, and by 1824 the British had negotiated a second agreement in which they acquired the island outright. By the 1870s, Singapore had become a major port in the region, as well as one of the most prosperous cities. The population grew, and more Europeans poured in. Singapore enjoyed peaceful times until the Japanese invaded in December, 1941. The Japanese occupation lasted until the end of World War II, after which the country returned to British rule. In 1948, the Communist Party of Malaya attempted to take over Singapore, resulting in a state of emergency that lasted for 12 years. This led to the British decision to grant Singapore greater self-government, and finally, democratic elections in 1955. However, full self-government wasn't achieved until 1959. Since then, Singapore politics have been marked by struggles with potential communist takeovers and a short-lived merger with Malaya, Sarawak, and North Borneo from 1963-1965. In December, 1965, Singapore became a republic, although still under the protection of the British Empire. This protection was removed by 1971, and Singapore became fully self-sufficient. In August, 1967, the Association of Southeast Nations was formed, with Singapore, Indonesia, Malaysia, the Philippines, and Thailand as its first members.

Today Singapore is a thriving republic with a parliamentary government headed by a prime minister and a cabinet, as well as a president who is head of state. It is a major investor in Southeast Asia.

Statistics and Information

Air Travel

Singapore's Changi Airport is one of the most modern and convenient in the world. It offers numerous services and a free trolley to help you with your baggage.

If your hotel does not offer a limo or bus service, there are plenty of public taxis and buses (it's a 20-minute drive into the city). Taxi fares range from $20 to $30.

Country Code

Singapore's country code is 65.

When you are in Singapore and would like to call another country, dial 055, followed by the country code, the town code minus the first 0, and then the subscriber number.

To call Singapore from another country, dial the IDD access code (for example, 010 in Great Britain and 011 in the United States), followed by Singapore's country code and then the subscriber number.

Currency

The *Singapore dollar* (abbreviated S$) is the currency. Coins are issued in 1, 5, 10, 20, 50, and 100 *cents*. Notes are issued in units of S$1, 2, 5, 10, 20, 50, 100, 500, 1,000, and 10,000.

Money-changers will actually provide a better exchange rate than banks. Money-changers are available in shopping areas. However, the place where you will receive the best exchange rate is called Change Alley, where you can find money-changers and vendors of tobacco, newspapers, and so on. If you choose to make your exchange at a hotel, expect to pay a commission that is 5-percent higher than what you will pay at banks or through money-changers.

When exchanging traveler's checks for this country's currency, be sure to have your passport—you will need it for identification.

Dates

Dates are written with the day preceding the month, and then the year. January 30, 1999, would be written 30/1/99.

Ethnic Makeup

Singapore is a multi-ethnic society. Nearly three quarters of the population are Chinese, and approximately 14 percent are Malays, while less than 10 percent are Indians. A very small segment of the population consists of Arabs, Jews, and Armenians.

Holidays

The following are the holidays that are celebrated throughout Singapore and in specific sections of the country. It is wise to avoid scheduling meetings during these times.

January 1	New Year's Day
Early Friday in April	Good Friday
May 1	Labor Day
June/July	Hari Raya Haji (a holy day for Muslims, celebrating the pilgrimage to Mecca; celebrated according to the lunar calendar)

August 9	National Day
October/ November	Deepavali (celebrates the triumph of Krishna over the demon king, Nasakasura; celebrated according to the lunar calendar)
December 25	Christmas Day

Languages

With the multi-ethnic individuals who make up this country, it's no wonder that Singapore has four official languages: English, Chinese, Malay, and Tamil. When children are schooled, they are required to learn English and the language of their heritage. If their parents represent two different nationalities, the child is required to learn the language of his or her father's ancestors.

Note: The colloquial English that you may hear may be a variation of the English to which you are accustomed. It is called *Singlish*, which is a combination of words and rules from both the Singaporean language and English.

Religion

Singapore's residents practice a variety of religions. Buddhist, Muslim, Christian, and Hindu are the most popular.

Time Zone Differences

Singapore is eight hours ahead of Greenwich Mean Time and 13 hours ahead of U.S. Eastern Standard Time.

Weather

Singapore has a tropical climate. Temperatures are hot (mid-70s through mid-90s) and there is a lot of rain year-round.

Etiquette

Business Attire

Professionalism in both dress and demeanor are appropriate for women at all times. Skirts that are at the knee or below are considered appropriate, as are blouses with sleeves, business suits, and high-quality pant suits.

While short sleeves may be appropriate for men when it is very hot and humid, a long-sleeve white shirt and suit or a sport coat and trousers are preferred.

Business-card Etiquette

Business cards should be exchanged with every business associate you meet. Bring plenty of cards with you, because this is an important part of developing relationships.

Note that there is a ritual to exchanging business cards with Chinese Singaporeans. First, using both hands, offer a card to the other person so that he or she can see your name clearly, without having to turn it around to read it. In turn, you should accept the other person's business card with two hands. Look at the card for a few seconds and then back at the person who offered it to you, as though you are making the association between the person and the information on the card. Finally, put the card away in your business card case if you are standing or place it on the table in front of you if you are sitting.

Business Entertaining/Dining

When doing business in Singapore, you will find that much time is spent establishing rapport. This is done primarily around meals: lunch, dinner, and banquets. If your Chinese client has arranged a banquet in your honor during your stay, be sure to reciprocate before leaving Singapore.

When you are setting up a meal, be aware of the foods that may be considered taboo by your Singaporean client. In most cases, you will be able to determine this based on the person's cultural heritage.

For example, your Singaporean Chinese client may prefer foods that are spicy; your Muslim client will not drink alcohol; and your Buddhist client will not eat beef.

Toasting: You will know that the meal has officially begun when the host invites you to sip your beverage. A common ritual will be for your host to raise his or her own glass and say the equivalent of "please" or *ch'ing*. In turn, you should raise your glass with both hands (your right hand under the bottom of the glass and your left hand supporting the glass). As you partake in the toast, you should join those around you by saying, "to success" in Chinese (*yam seng*). At that point, you should sip the beverage by holding it with only your right hand.

After the first sip is taken, your Chinese host will give you the signal to eat by lifting his or her chopsticks horizontally and saying, *ch'ing* again. If your host has not already done so, he or she will then serve you. It will be up to you to officially begin the meal by taking the first bite.

Prepare to use chopsticks if you are in a Chinese restaurant. You will also be presented with several bowls—for rice, for soup, for bones, and for sauces. Unlike the custom in Hong Kong, a napkin will also be available.

As in Hong Kong, the food will be served on a revolving tray (similar to a lazy Susan). Be mindful of the host's responsibility to replenish the food on the plate of each guest; this is something you should do when you are hosting a meal.

When guests are serving themselves, they should make a point of taking only the piece of food closest to them. Search for the largest piece of food only if you are hosting the meal and wish to find the best piece of food for your guest of honor.

When entertaining Singaporean clients, make a point of thinking like they do. For example, to most Westerners, the white meat of the chicken is considered the best part, whereas the dark meat is considered to be the best to Singaporeans. This is therefore the part you should serve.

It is a high honor to be served a whole chicken or fish. This signifies that your host did not skimp by offering you only a piece of the animal.

You will discover that vegetables are served cooked rather than in the form of raw appetizers or salads. When entertaining your Singaporean client in your country, be sure to offer vegetables according to how they are accustomed to eating them.

Chopsticks should be rested (on the chopstick rest) after every few bites. They should also be resting when you are taking a sip of a beverage or talking.

It is appropriate to refuse a second portion of a food until the host asks you a few times.

Note that Singaporeans do not drink water with a meal.

Although tea is consumed as part of some Asian meals, this is not the case in Singapore. Instead, it will be offered to you before a meal and following it.

Alcohol and beer are common beverages that may be served with a meal. When ordering a beer, be aware that it may be served with ice in it. If you prefer a nonalcoholic beverage, simply make that request.

When eating soup, you should use the spoon that was provided to you. While it is considered in bad form to lift the soup to sip it, slurping soup from the spoon is considered acceptable.

As in Hong Kong, if you are served fish, do not turn the plate, but eat it in the position in which it was presented to you.

If you have something in your mouth that you would like to remove, it is more appropriate to use your chopsticks rather than your hands. The undesirable food should be placed either on the small plate that was given to you for this type of situation or on the tablecloth if a plate was not offered to you.

Rather than telling your Chinese hosts that you cannot stomach a particular food, it would be better to tell the person that you may not eat it for health reasons.

As in China, Saudi Arabia, and some other Middle Eastern countries, a belch signifies that the person has been satisfied with the meal.

When eating with Malays and Indians, rather than using chopsticks, your eating utensils will be a spoon and a fork, and you may sometimes also use your right hand. The spoon is the utensil that should be put in your mouth, while the fork is for scooping the food onto your spoon.

Indian utensil etiquette dictates that the serving spoon should not touch the plate when either you or another person is putting food on a plate.

There is no lingering at the end of a meal. Rather, it is time to leave after the last course has been finished, or after tea has been served.

Conversation

Safe topics of conversation include the variety of foods available in Singapore, the sights you have visited, and the arts.

While it is considered gauche for Westerners to ask each other questions about age, weight, salary, and so on, these are topics that you might be asked about in Singapore. You can allow the questioner to save face by simply evading the questions with as much grace as possible. Just don't express offense.

Topics to avoid include another individual's personal life, personal status, and so on. As in most other countries, religion, politics, and other controversial subjects should be avoided. You will be safe if you follow the conversational leads that have already been established by the questions that have been asked of you.

As in many Arab countries, paying a compliment to another person may be misinterpreted as your having a hidden agenda or romantic interest. It is therefore better to compliment a person on his or her accomplishments, rather than on his or her personal appearance.

To Westerners, effective listening dictates that you "count to two" or pause after someone has said something to you, as a way of allowing the person to finish his or her train of thought and also to avoid interruptions. However, Singaporean listening etiquette dictates that you count to 10 before responding. By waiting a minimum of 10 seconds, you will demonstrate that you have given thought to what you heard before responding.

Gestures and Public Manners

Important: The Singaporean government has a very low crime rate, due in no small part to its very strict law enforcement. People who do not abide by the law are fined and sometimes even put in jail. Bear this in mind when you visit, as there are things you would do in your own country that you simply shouldn't do in Singapore! This includes jaywalking, chewing gum, smoking in public, spitting, and not flushing a toilet.

When you need a taxi, it's best to go to a stand where queues or lines are formed. If you want to catch a taxi without standing in line, you can take your chances by standing somewhere that looks safe (that is, away from heavy traffic) and waiting for a cab to stop. If you see that an empty taxi does not stop for you, don't take offense; the driver may be on his way to pick up another person or may be ending his workday. If a driver acknowledges you as he passes by moving his hand, it is a sign that he is off duty for a while.

Be sure to carry little packs of tissues with you. They will come in handy if you enter a public rest room that is without tissue. Note that some public rest rooms will have toilets that will allow you to "sit down" while others will require that you "squat."

When pointing, do so with an open hand, rather than with your index finger.

Avoid touching or patting someone. This is seen as a demeaning gesture.

Speak in an "indoor" voice, with lowered tones; do not shout.

Public displays of affection are taboo. That includes a couple holding hands or even kissing when meeting or departing. However, if you see two women holding hands, don't be surprised. This gesture is a sign of friendship.

While Westerners consider eye contact to be a sign of listening, that is not the case in Singapore. Instead, it is considered polite to break eye contact so that you do not seem to be staring or glaring at the person.

A smile can have many different interpretations. You will see Singaporeans smile when they are happy, when they find something funny, and when they are embarrassed, upset, or even unhappy.

Gift-giving Etiquette

As in other Asian countries, giving and receiving gifts are part of the ritual of establishing and maintaining relationships. A large gift should be presented to an entire group. When giving small gifts, they should be given to everyone in attendance in order to allow everyone to save face and maintain harmony.

Appropriate gifts include something from your city, items with your company logo on it, and higher-end gifts with brand names that are recognizable. Gifts should be given in pairs to your Singaporean client of Chinese descent because even numbers are considered to be good luck. However, if you are visiting the home of a Singaporean of Indian heritage, be sure to do the reverse by giving gifts in uneven numbers, which are considered good fortune to Indians.

Whatever you do, avoid giving clocks, cutlery, scissors, flowers, and hankies. A clock is considered a sign of bad luck, cutlery and scissors are thought of as severing ties, and flowers and hankies are thought of as something that you take to funerals.

Whenever you are invited to the home of a Singaporean, be sure to go with something in hand (sweets or some other dessert, for example). Be sure to take either an even or uneven amount of dessert, depending on the nationality of your Singaporean client.

When giving gifts to your Chinese or Indian client, appropriate colors of gift wrap are red, pink, and gold. Colors to avoid are black, navy, and white, which are equated with death and mourning. Your Malay client will appreciate a gift wrapped in red or green paper.

When you are offered a gift, refuse it a few times before accepting it. This gesture displays your humility and says that you are unworthy of receiving it. When you finally accept it, be sure not to open it until you are alone. Conversely, when you are giving a gift, you can expect for the gift to be refused two or three times before it is accepted, and your Singaporean client will not open it in front of you.

Greetings and Introductions

The Chinese way: When meeting a Singaporean of Chinese descent, remember that the first name you hear will be the last name or family name, while the second name will be the given name or first name. When you are being introduced to someone with a title or a high-ranking position, you should use the title during your greeting (for example, President Chan, Dr. Abdallah).

The Malay way: Rather than using a last name, etiquette dictates that individuals of Malay descent use their first names followed by the equivalent of "son of" (*bin*) or "daughter of" (*binti*) and their father's first name. For example, Abdullah *bin* Yusif is Abdullah, the son of Yusif; Yasmeen *binti* Yusif is Yasmeen, the daughter of Yusif.

The Indian way: Just as with individuals of Malay descent, Singaporeans of Indian descent who speak Tamil do not use surnames. Rather, the initial of the father's first name is used before the person's first name (for example, J. Manish). When you address the person, you should use "Mr. Manish." When a woman marries, it is customary for her to substitute the initial representing her father's given name with that of her husband's given name.

When shaking hands, expect a lighter grip than you would from a Westerner. Follow suit by shaking hands in the same manner. As in most countries, etiquette dictates that you stand to shake hands, both when meeting someone and also at the end of the gathering, as one of you is preparing to depart. A distance of approximately two arm's lengths should be maintained.

When shaking hands with a Singaporean, prepare for a two-handed handshake. Your handshake should also take longer than a few quick, firm pumps. It should be light, lingering, and last around a quarter of a minute.

What Westerners consider small talk is really a greeting in Singapore. For instance, when someone asks a Westerner, "How are you?" or "How's business?" the person may respond, "Great, thanks." However, when you are meeting with Singaporeans and you are asked, "How's business?" your response should be a humble one, such as, "It's moderate"—even if it is great. It will always behoove you to display humility, no matter how much business is booming.

Meeting Manners

When scheduling or accepting invitations to meetings, make sure that you are clear about the meeting date, which can be misunderstood if written in numbers (12/11/99, for example). Because of the British influence in Singapore, the day is listed before the month, which is followed by the year. For that reason, if a Singaporean asks if you can meet on 12/11/99, the person is requesting that you meet on November 12, 1999, not December 11, 1999.

While many Westerners would not think twice about staying seated when their parents or managers entered a room, this is not the case in Singapore. Here are just a few rules of etiquette to follow for displaying deference to parents, grandparents, and older relatives, as well as those above you from a hierarchical standpoint:

- Stand when family members more than one generation older than you enter a room. Also follow this rule of respect when your manager or someone higher in rank than you enters a room.

- Always wait for the individuals described in the previous rule to begin eating before you do.

- When sitting in a chair, keep your feet flat on the floor, rather than crossing your legs in front of elders or hierarchical superiors.

- Avoid challenging, correcting, or disagreeing with an elder person or superior in a public setting. Besides causing them to lose face, you will lose the respect of others. (Note: This rule should also be followed when you are with your boss and are in a meeting with Singaporeans). Similarly, if you are taking a course and would like to pose a question to your teacher, it would be more appropriate to do so in private after class, rather than in front of the entire group.

- Refrain from facial expressions that show you disagree (such as frowning at something you may disagree with or shaking your head no).

- Keep your cool and refrain from showing that you are upset. By staying calm, you will be perceived as being able to control your emotions, rather than allowing them to control you.

A Singaporean may actually mean "yes" when he or she:

- Says "perhaps."

- Agrees to your proposition and then offers to be of assistance to you.

- Says yes and then asks you a related question about what he or she has agreed to do.

Here are some phrases that may sound like "yes," but may mean "no" to a Singaporean:

- "It may not work out."

- "My schedule may not permit me..."

- "Yes, but..."

Punctuality

While it is considered appropriate to be on time, once in a while a Singaporean may choose to arrive a few minutes late so as not to appear overly anxious, especially if the person has been invited to a function in which food will be served.

Seating Etiquette

Most likely, you will sit at a round table with an even number of guests if your host is a Singaporean Chinese (even numbers signify good luck). While Western etiquette dictates that the host sit to the immediate left of the guest, the opposite is true in Singapore. Your host will sit to the immediate right of the most senior guest.

If your host is of Malay descent, he will offer you either the seat to his right or the head of the table.

Tipping Tips

It is customary not to tip hotel doormen, cab drivers, and so on. In fact, in some cases, signs will be posted encouraging you not to tip.

As in many other countries, a 10- to 15-percent surcharge will be built into a restaurant bill. If you notice that a surcharge is not built into your bill, add 10 to 15 percent to the total. In addition, if someone has performed an extra service for you (such as delivered or picked up something from your hotel room) a S$1 to S$2 tip is in order.

When You Are Invited to a Singaporean Home

It is customary to remove your shoes before entering a house, although sometimes your hosts may tell you that it is not necessary to do so. To be sure, take a look at what they are doing. If their shoes are removed and they are either barefoot or are wearing slippers, you should follow suit. Note: Be sure that your socks are in good shape.

Women in Business

Western women doing business in Singapore should realize that it is not common for men and women to interact as colleagues in the same way that they do in the United States. For that reason, women may want to set the tone by initiating a handshake, rather than waiting for a Singaporean man to do so. If women do not initiate the handshake, they will be acknowledged by men with a nod and a smile.

Maintaining at least a 10- to 15-inch distance is considered appropriate when men and women are interacting as colleagues.

Note: Women should not enter a temple when menstruating because it is considered taboo.

Whatever You Do...

- Don't chew gum. There is no room for mastication in Singapore. If you dispose of chewed gum in public, it will cost you S$500. If you are ever caught selling it, you will be fined S$2,000.

- Don't jaywalk. This offense will cost you S$20. To avoid paying it, use the bridges that pass over the busy streets; they have been specially built for pedestrian traffic.

- Don't take away the pedestrian's right of way if you are driving. If you don't cede the right of way to a pedestrian, you can be fined S$150.

- Don't be a litter bug. Most of us can think of spending S$1,000 on something other than being fined for throwing even the smallest bit of trash on the ground. To avoid such a fine, be sure to dispose of food wrappers, receipts, and other paper items in the cans designated for trash.

- Don't smoke in public places. If you are a smoker, think twice before you light up. Most places open to the public ban smoking. If you are caught puffing, expect to pay as much as S$1,000.

- Don't spit. Whoever is caught spitting in public will be fined as much as S$1,000.

- Don't walk away from a toilet without flushing it. Rather than flushing S$150 down the commode, flip that handle!

Chapter 10

South Korea

8 reasons people do business in South Korea

1. South Korea has the 11th largest economy in the world and is the sixth largest trading nation internationally.

2. South Korea is well-known for electronics manufacturing.

3. English is South Korea's primary business language.

4. South Korea's chief crops are rice, barley, and vegetables.

5. South Korea has numerous mineral reserves, including tungsten, coal, and graphite.

6. Clothing and textiles are among South Korea's strongest industries.

7. South Koreans have a strong work ethic, as well as one of the longest work weeks of any country across the globe.

8. South Korean businesspeople make good use of mediators for developing business relationships.

South Korea, also known as the Republic of Korea, is located on a peninsula in far eastern Asia, directly between China and Japan. Its southernmost point is within 70 miles of Japan's island of Kyushu, in the Korean strait. The Yellow Sea lies between South Korea and China. In addition to the peninsular mainland, South Korea also consists of more than 3,300 islands, of which only 300 or so are inhabited.

South Korea's land is marked by numerous mountain ranges and a rugged, rocky shoreline, but unlike Japan, it does not have much volcanic or other geologic activity. The land is abundant in granite and limestone, as well as rivers. South Korea was once heavily dependent on its rivers for trade and transportation, and many of its major cities, such as Seoul, are located on rivers.

The people of South Korea (population of more than 41 million) have an historical and cultural heritage going back more than 5,000 years. South Koreans place great value on family and respect for parents and elders. Seniority and hierarchy are an important part of the Korean way of life. South Korea also enjoys one of the highest literacy rates in the world.

Korea has long been a point of contention between China and Japan, and was colonized at one time by Japan. The colonization ended in 1945, at the conclusion of World War II. From 1950 to 1953, the people of Korea were subjected to a brutal war that resulted in the country's being divided into two parts: North Korea, controlled by the Communists, and South Korea, a free democracy. In time, South Korea became a major economic force in the modern world, and in 1988 hosted the 24th Olympic Games. South Korea became a member of the United Nations in 1991.

Note: Because North Korea remains closed to outside business, the focus of this chapter is on South Korea. However, the customs and manners that are discussed also reflect, for the most part, the traditions of North Korea.

Statistics and Information

Air Travel

Kimpo International Airport serves Seoul. There are many options for reaching your hotel upon arrival. Taxis are located in front of each terminal and charge a reasonable fare. Buses are also available and may be a less-expensive option.

Country Code

The country code for South Korea is 82.

Area codes for some major South Korean cities are:

- 0652 for Chonbuk.
- 032 for Inchon.
- 0361 for Kangwon.
- 0431 for Kwangju.
- 051 for Pusan.
- 02 for Seoul.
- 053 for Taegu.
- 042 for Taejon.

When you are in a country other than South Korea and would like to call one of the regions listed, simply dial the area codes without the 0 preceding it.

Currency

The currency in South Korea is the *won* (KW). A *won* is made up of 100 *chon*. Its notes are in denominations of KW10,000, 5,000, and 1,000. South Korean coins are made in KW500, 100, 50, 10, 5, and 1.

When you need to exchange money, be sure to visit a money-changer, either at a hotel or a department store. While you will also find money-changers at airports, and can also visit a bank to make transactions, you may save as much as 5 percent by exchanging your currency at a hotel or department store.

When exchanging traveler's checks for this country's currency, be sure to have your passport—you will need it for identification.

Dates

Because South Korean etiquette requires dates to be written by listing the year, month, and day (for example, 99/5/7), you will probably find it easy to confuse the month and day. Therefore, it is probably best to write dates out by spelling the month, day, and year in alphanumeric form (for example, May 7, 1999).

Ethnic Makeup

South Korea is a homogeneous society whose ancestry can be traced from Siberia, Manchuria, and Inner Mongolia. The people are largely descended from Mongol tribes.

Like Japan, South Korea maintains its own culture and customs, rather than blending with the customs and manners of other cultures (although there is some cultural interchange with China because of its proximity).

Holidays

The following are the holidays that are celebrated throughout the country. It is wise to avoid scheduling meetings during these times.

January 1-3	New Year's Day
January/February	Lunar New Year's Day

March 1	Independence Day
May	Buddha's Birthday (the date varies, depending on the lunar calendar)
May 5	Children's Day
June 6	Memorial Day
July 17	Constitution Day
August 15	Liberation Day
September/ October	Chusok (Korean Thanksgiving; the date varies, depending on the lunar calendar)
October 3	National Foundation Day
December 25	Christmas Day

Language

Korean is the national language of this country. It is considered to have been part of the Ural-Altaic group, with Mongolian and Manchurian influences.

Although there are no similarities between the Korean and Chinese languages, Chinese characters were used in the 15th century to invent the Korean alphabet (*hangul*). Finnish and Japanese grammar are also thought to have influenced the Korean language.

Religion

While Buddhism is the most widely practiced religion, Confucianism and Shamanism are also observed by many South Koreans. In addition, more than 40 percent of the population is comprised of Christians.

Time Zone Differences

South Korea is nine hours ahead of Greenwich Mean Time and 14 hours ahead of U.S. Eastern Standard Time.

Weather

As in the United States, South Korea has four seasons. Spring is short (April-May), and temperatures are usually in the mid-50s Fahrenheit. During the summer months (June-August), temperatures can reach the mid-90s. Monsoons are very common during this season, with typhoons sometimes occurring at the end of summer. Temperatures in the fall (September-October) range between the 30s and the mid-60s. Winters are long (November-March), cold, and dry, with temperatures ranging between the teens and the 30s.

Etiquette

Business Attire

Conservative business dress is considered appropriate in South Korea. For men that means a dark suit, white shirt, and tie. Women should wear a suit or business dress rather than slacks. Blouses with sleeves and skirts in a conservative length should be worn in lieu of sleeveless tops and miniskirts.

When you are invited to business/social functions (such as sports outings), it is also important to dress appropriately. Ask someone who uses good judgment and has attended these types of functions for advice on what to wear in these instances.

Avoid shorts or similarly casual attire; such clothing should be left at home.

Business-card Etiquette

As in other Asian countries, your business cards—also called name cards—are an important part of establishing long-term relationships.

You will be judged according to the role you play in your organization. Your title should therefore be emphasized on your business card. This is because 1) it gives the person receiving the card an idea of your job responsibility; 2) it assists him or her in determining the amount of decision-making authority you have; and 3) it assists your contact in matching you with a person who is of similar rank. This last reason is probably the most important one for emphasizing your title on your card.

Because you will exchange your business card with nearly everyone you meet, take many more with you than you typically exchange with Westerners. In fact, many business travelers have found that they can never have too many. For that reason, they pack an entire box of cards (about 500 cards), because they realize that it's much easier to return to their own country with extra cards than to lose face and be without cards while they are meeting and greeting others.

You need to be sure that your cards can be easily read by the South Koreans with whom you will be meeting. One way to do this is to have them translated into Korean. This arrangement can be made with the hotel concierge or a person in the business center who can have your cards translated within a short period of time.

Take care of your cards, because the business card exchange is a very important way of beginning the relationship-building process. A business card case will allow you to keep your cards clean and crisp. It also will allow you to have a specific place to put another person's card after it has been received and studied for a few minutes.

Business Entertaining/Dining

Entertaining during meals and developing friendships is a very important part of developing relationships with South Koreans. It is an opportunity to be with individuals in an informal environment so that you can establish rapport and get to know each other on a more personal basis. Thus, when invitations are extended to you, they should be accepted and should also be reciprocated within a reasonable amount of time during your visit.

Leave spouses behind. While it is common in other countries to extend dinner invitations to spouses, this is not the case when interacting with South Koreans. Business entertaining is reserved for the parties responsible for negotiations.

Rather than being presented with everything at once, South Korean dining consists of several small courses served one after the other. Be prepared: Many dishes are very spicy!

Prepare to enjoy rice as the foundation of each meal. This staple will be served with fish, beef, chicken, or pork, which may be marinated and grilled at your table, then served in slices rolled in lettuce with rice and a bean paste.

Kimchi is a spicy cabbage dish that is commonly served in South Korea. It is eaten with sticky rice and may vary to include seaweed, roots, and radishes. After enjoying *kimchi*, Koreans encourage that hot tea be taken. One reason is that it assists in cleansing the palate so that you can better enjoy the tastes of other foods to follow.

Eat rather than talk. While conversation is important for becoming acquainted, lengthy discussions are best saved for either before or after the meal.

Rather than waiting for the host to put food on your plate, you may do so yourself.

As in other situations, always use your right hand to both pass and receive items at the table. If you would like to show added respect for someone, allow your left hand to support your right arm when offering an item to that person at the table.

Practice using chopsticks before your trip to South Korea because they are the most commonly used utensils. You will also be offered a spoon for eating soups and dishes with noodles.

Drinking is a very important part of establishing relationships. For that reason, expect to be offered greater amounts of alcohol than you ordinarily would on the Western front. Note that Scotch is a very popular drink in South Korea.

When you are in a business-entertaining environment and have been served a drink, get ready for a toast to be made. The most common South Korean toast you will hear is *Gun-hei*. When you lift your goblet, be sure to do so with your right hand. To display added respect to the person being toasted, support your right arm with your left hand.

While it is considered good manners in other countries to leave something in your glass if you would like it replenished, this is not the case in South Korea. Rather, when you drink all of it, this acts as a cue to your host that you would like your glass to be refilled.

If you are a man and prefer not to consume any alcoholic beverages, you can save face for yourself and those around you by saying that you are declining to drink for "health reasons" or "religious reasons."

It is considered more appropriate for females not to drink than to consume alcohol. For that reason, women should stick with sodas or juices.

Conversation

Topics that are appropriate to discuss with South Koreans include the country's economic success and international accomplishments, sports, personal hobbies, and family.

One way that South Koreans believe they can establish rapport with others is by finding common denominators. This is one of the reasons that you may be asked questions that might be considered inappropriate in your own country (for example, your age, salary, marital status, religious beliefs, etc.).

Answer questions affirmatively and in the most positive way, even when you have to deliver negative information.

Be concise and direct in your response. When you are asked a question, remember that "less is more," so don't overelaborate.

Tone down hand motions and facial expressions when talking. Avoid being too animated, as this is not accepted practice in South Korea.

Topics to avoid: The Korean War, communism, Korean politics, your recent visit to Japan.

Gestures and Public Manners

Maintain harmony at all costs. Like Thais, South Koreans tend to smile a lot. This is partly because of the teachings of Confucius, which encourages appropriate form and harmony at all times. By the same token, any form of criticism should be done in private rather than out in the open.

Avoid touching someone on the back or even on the person's arm. Any form of physical contact is considered disrespectful.

When complimenting a South Korean, expect your comment to be accepted with humility, perhaps even denied.

If a South Korean appears reserved when you first meet, it may be because you have not yet established rapport. Time and trust are needed to allow relationships to develop, thus making it possible for individuals to feel more comfortable with one another.

Queuing doesn't exist. While South Koreans are very form-oriented in personal situations, this is not the case when they are standing in line in public places. In fact, it is quite common to push and shove in public.

When offering or receiving something, be sure to do so with your right hand. If you would like to display deference to the person, allow your left hand to support your right elbow while holding out or taking the object. Additional respect for a more senior individual may be demonstrated by allowing your left fingers to touch your right wrist as you are offering the object.

Sometimes you will be required to remove your shoes before entering a room or other location. For that reason, be sure that your socks are clean and neat.

When talking or laughing, keep your voice as quiet as possible. South Koreans tend to speak in a soft voice, and you will want to keep your tones harmonious with theirs.

If you have to blow your nose, be sure to do so in private. This is considered a vulgar gesture.

Like anyone else, South Koreans laugh when something is funny. They may also laugh when they are embarrassed. You should follow the South Korean habit of covering your mouth when you laugh.

Gift-giving Etiquette

While it is not necessary to take a gift to a meeting, it certainly will be appreciated if you are traveling from your home country and are meeting for the first time. Appropriate gifts include an item with your organization's logo, something that is commemorative of your city, etc. Your gift should be of good quality, yet not so expensive that you embarrass the receiver.

When you give a gift, do not expect the person to open it in front of you. It is considered more appropriate for the receiver to open a present in private.

When you receive a gift, you should wait to open it in private, even if the person giving it to you encourages you to open it in front of him or her. The only time you should break this rule is if you have given the person a gift and he or she chooses to open it with you present.

When you know you will be giving a gift to several people within an organization, be sure to give a gift of greater value to the senior person. The gifts you present to that person's subordinates may be similar, as long as they are of lesser value than the one you give their superior.

While your gift will demonstrate your thoughtfulness, where it was made is of utmost importance. Whatever you do, be sure your gift was made in your own country rather than in Japan or South Korea.

If you receive a dragon as a gift, consider it a compliment. South Koreans consider dragons to be signs of respect and good luck, as well as a way of keeping away evil spirits.

Greetings and Introductions

A South Korean greeting consists of bending your upper body a little when meeting another person. This gesture may also be made as you are shaking hands with someone. When you would like to demonstrate added respect, allow your left hand to support your right arm.

Rather than waiting for a senior person to bow, South Korean etiquette dictates that a junior person initiate this gesture. A senior person may choose to extend his hand first if he wishes to set the tone of the greeting with a junior. With both types of greetings, prolonged eye contact should be avoided by both parties.

While it is acceptable for a woman from the Western hemisphere to initiate a handshake with a South Korean man, it is more appropriate to allow a South Korean woman to initiate a handshake. If she does not extend a hand, she may nod as a greeting.

Your reputation is based on the person who introduced you. When you are ready to begin establishing relationships with a South Korean company, be sure to find a "go-between" to help introduce you to the appropriate people in that company. Besides saving a lot of time, you will be thought of with the same respect as the person who helped you with the introduction.

(See also Business-card Etiquette.)

Meeting Manners

It is part of the South Korean meeting ritual to begin by offering guests a beverage. Accept a drink when it's offered to you, even if you only choose to sip rather than drink it.

Be patient and wait before getting down to business. Meetings always begin with small talk. Rather than "cutting to the chase," let the person with whom you are meeting set the tone about when business discussions should begin.

If a South Korean is bothered or confused by something that has been said, he or she will likely not express this concern verbally, but instead will expect you to know it from his or her body language or facial expression. Concern may also be expressed by sucking in air through the teeth. Thus, if any individuals at a meeting look even slightly confused about something that has been said during your presentation, or if you hear the air-sucking sound, be sure to ask for questions. You also may try to clarify what you have said by rephrasing it.

When planning meetings with South Koreans, be sure to build in several breaks for smoking. Smoking is very common in South Korea, so this courtesy will be much appreciated. (Note: If you are meeting at a nonsmoking site in your own country, be sure to provide locations where smoking is allowed.)

Prepare your presentation so that your South Korean meeting participants will be encouraged to ask questions. In addition, while South Koreans may read and write English, they may be less proficient in understanding the spoken word. For that reason, it is wise to provide documentation for what you will be presenting. This will assist the individuals present in following along and getting a clear picture of your presentation, thus enabling them to share it with higher-ups who may not be present.

If your contacts do not speak for what you may consider a long period of time (15 to 30 seconds), do not misinterpret this as a sign of their not being interested in what you said. Most likely, they are giving careful thought to what they've just heard.

When you hear a "yes," be sure not to misinterpret it to mean that "the deal is in the bag." Frequently, an affirmative answer means "I hear what you are saying" or "I understand." South Koreans are firm believers in helping others to save face by not putting them in embarrassing situations.

Punctuality

South Korean businesspersons, especially top executives, are extremely busy and their hectic schedules may cause them to be a few minutes late for appointments. However, Westerners should always be on time.

Seating Etiquette

The best seat (usually the center seat facing the door) should always be offered to the most senior person present in the room.

Tipping Tips

As in many other Asian countries, a service charge is automatically included in restaurant and hotel bills. For that reason, tipping is not necessary unless someone has provided you with exceptional service that you feel merits an additional reward. When this is the case, the most appropriate tip is 10 percent.

While cab drivers do not expect to be tipped, they certainly appreciate receiving any extra gratuity. One common way to tip cab drivers is to let them keep any extra change left over after paying your fare. As with restaurant and hotel personnel, if the driver assists you in any other way (with luggage, for example), it is good manners to give the person approximately 10 percent of your fare.

When You Are Invited to a South Korean Home

South Koreans enjoy entertaining guests in their homes. Invitations are informal and may be extended only hours before you are to arrive. Being a few minutes late in arriving is acceptable.

Because eating, sitting, and even sleeping are done on the floor in Korea, it is imperative that the floor remain clean. Remove your shoes before entering the house and put on house slippers if your host provides them.

Westerners will find it unusual that the hostess will most likely not join the party for the meal; she will be in the kitchen preparing food or overseeing servants. She may join you at the end of the evening for singing and drinks.

Women in Business

South Koreans are much more used to interacting with men in decision-making roles. Women may find certain situations awkward or uncomfortable because of this.

Whatever You Do...

- Don't be surprised if you meet several people at once with the last name of "Kim." Believe it or not, nearly a quarter of the population has this as a last name.

- Don't misinterpret what you said as having been funny if your South Korean colleague laughs. South Koreans also laugh when they are uncomfortable or embarrassed.

- Don't wear bright colors. Conservative colors are considered more appropriate.

- Don't tip as you do in your own country. Tipping everyone who has rendered a service for you is unnecessary.

- Don't assume that a South Korean man will introduce his wife using his last name. Married women retain their surnames and are addressed by "Mrs." and that name.

- Don't use chopsticks when eating rice. South Korean etiquette dictates that a metal spoon be used.

- Don't be surprised if you see people on the street wearing surgical masks. It means that they have a cold and are trying not to spread germs.

Advice From the Experts

"When you are in business situations, do not become 'chummy.' Respectful behavior between individuals is vital. Also, always match the rank of the individual you are dealing with in negotiations."

—*A vice president of a national materials manufacturing organization*

Chapter 11

Taiwan

---

8 reasons people do business in Taiwan

1. Taiwan is a world leader in the manufacture of electronics.

2. Taiwan's other manufacturing strengths are in textiles and clothing.

3. Taiwan has an abundance of marble, coal, and limestone.

4. This country's chief crops are vegetables, rice, and fruit.

5. Taiwan is an economic powerhouse in the region.

6. It is on the top 10 list for both importing and exporting.

7. Taiwan's language for doing business is English.

8. Taiwanese businesspeople have an entrepreneurial spirit and a very strong work ethic.

Taiwan is an island nation located in the Pacific Ocean, approximately 100 miles southeast from the Chinese coast. It is situated between Korea and Japan on the north and Hong Kong and the Philippines on the south. This puts it in a strategic location in Southeast Asia as a natural gateway to other countries. Taiwan's principal city is Taipei.

The island is 245 miles long and 89.5 miles wide at the broadest point. Approximately two thirds of the country is made up of mountains and forests, with the remainder being foothills and plains. Despite its relatively small size, Taiwan is one of the most densely populated countries in the world, with a population of well over 20 million people. Of these, approximately 350,000 are aborigines; the remainder are immigrants from the Chinese mainland.

Taiwan first came under Chinese control in the 1200s and was declared a province of China in 1885. For several centuries, it was known in the west as Formosa, a name given to it by Portuguese traders meaning "The Beautiful." The island was occupied by European settlers for some time, including the Dutch and the Spanish, until the Europeans were driven out by the Chinese in the late 1600s. In 1884 to 1885, the French occupied northern Taiwan, but withdrew on agreement with China. In 1895, following the first Sino-Japanese War, China lost both Taiwan and the Pescadores archipelago to the Japanese, until the end of World War II when they were returned to the Chinese.

In 1911, the Republic of China was founded under the leadership of Generalissimo Chiang Kai-shek as a result of an uprising against the Ching dynasty. When his armies lost control of the country to Mao Zedong's Communist Party, Chiang and his followers retreated to Taiwan in 1949 and set up their nationalist government there, with Taipei established as the capitol. Subsequently Japan renounced all claims to the island.

For many years, the government of Taiwan, which has always declared itself to be the only legitimate Chinese administration, enjoyed the support and protection of the United States, which prevented an invasion from the mainland in 1953. However, as U.S. relations with Communist China began to improve in later years, Taiwan was eventually ousted from its seat in the United Nations and given over to the People's Republic of China. This led to divisions between the Chinese immigrants and native Taiwanese who wished to normalize relations with the mainland. After martial law was lifted in 1987, a movement began to grow to unify the island with the mainland. As of today, Taiwan is an independent nation, maintaining its own sovereignty. Nevertheless, China and Taiwan each claim sovereignty over the other.

Statistics and Information

Air Travel

Taiwan has two international airports: Chiang Kai-Shek Memorial International Airport, located in Taoyuan (approximately 25 miles from Taipei), and Kaohsiung International Airport, situated on the southwest tip of Taiwan.

From Chiang Kai-Shek Airport, transportation options vary. While limousine service is provided by the larger hotels, taxi service is also available. A bus line also goes directly from the airport to Taipei.

Country Code

The Taiwanese country code is 886.

The codes for the major cities are:

• 7 for Kaohsiung.

- 32 for Keelung.
- 4 for Taichung.
- 6 for Tainan.
- 2 for Taipei.

Currency

The NT$ (or the equivalent of 100 cents) is the symbol for the *New Taiwan dollar*. This currency is also called the *yuan*. The NT$ is available in denominations of 10, 50, 500, and 1,000. In addition, coins are available in denominations of 50 cents (NT$0.50), one dollar (NT$1), and five dollars (NT$5).

Currency exchange rates are among the best at Taiwan's airports. Therefore, it is a good idea to exchange some money before leaving the airport.

You will not find money-changers in Taiwan. Once you are in a city, your best bet for changing currency will be at a bank. If you find that a hotel is more convenient, the commission you pay will be only slightly higher than what you would pay at a bank.

When exchanging traveler's checks for this country's currency, be sure to have your passport—you will need it for identification.

Dates

As in South Korea, the proper way to write a date is by first listing the year followed by the month and then the day. However, when writing the year in Taiwan, it should be dated from when the Chinese republic began, in 1911, rather than beginning with 1900. In other words, July 5, 1999, should be written as 88/7/5.

Ethnic Makeup

More than three quarters of Taiwan's population are native Taiwanese originally from or descended from mainland Chinese. More than 10 percent are Hakkas and a very small percentage are aborigines of Polynesian/Malay descent.

Holidays

The following are the holidays that are celebrated throughout the country. It is wise to avoid scheduling meetings during these times.

January 1	National Founding Day of the Republic of China
January/ February	Chinese Lunar New Year (the date varies, depending on the lunar calendar)
February 6	Lantern Festival
March 29	Youth Day
April 5	Tomb Sweeping Day and Chiang Kai-shek's Memorial Festival
June	Dragon Boat Festival (the date varies, depending on the lunar calendar)
September	Mid-Autumn Moon Festival (the date varies, depending on the lunar calendar)
September 28	The Birthday of Confucius
October 10	Double Tenth National Day
October 25	Taiwan Restoration Day
October 31	Birthday of President Chiang Kai-shek
November 12	Birthday of Dr. Sun Yat-sen
December 25	Constitution Day

Language

While Mandarin is the official language in Taiwan, Taiwanese and other dialects are frequently heard. Individuals who are educated in Taiwan also learn English.

Religion

Buddhism and Taoism are the principal religions of Taiwan. Most of the population practices a combination of Buddhism, Taoism,

Christianity, and Islam. Confucianism is followed more as a code of ethics than as a religion.

Time Zone Differences

Taiwan is:

- Eight hours ahead of Greenwich Mean Time.
- 13 hours ahead of U.S. Eastern Standard Time.
- Two hours behind Australian Eastern Time.

Weather

Taiwan has tropical and subtropical weather. Winters are very mild, with temperatures in the mid-50s to 60s Fahrenheit, while its Spring and Autumn temperatures can vary from the high 50s to as high as the mid-80s. Summers tend to be hot and humid, with temperatures in the 80s and 90s. Note that summer is also typhoon season in Taiwan.

Etiquette

Business Attire

When visiting Taiwan, be sure to leave your business casual clothes at home. Professional, conservative attire is best.

Men should wear dark suits with ties, while women should wear business suits and dresses. Contrary to what would be considered appropriate attire in the United States, it is acceptable for men to wear short-sleeved shirts when it is extremely hot, but only if a first meeting has already taken place.

Pant suits may be considered by the Taiwanese to be business casual, so women should stick to skirts. Modesty is also valued, so women should be conscientious of appropriate necklines and skirt lengths.

Red, white, and black colors should be avoided.

Business-card Etiquette

As in other Asian countries, it is important to carry an ample supply of business cards because you will exchange them with everyone to whom you are formally introduced, regardless of position and rank. For this reason, be sure to take two or three times the number of cards you would normally carry with you. If you do not have a card to present to Taiwanese business associates, you will be perceived as rude and unprofessional.

It is wise to have your cards translated into Mandarin on the reverse side.

The way a business card is presented is as important a part of your introduction as anything else. Be sure to present your card with both hands and have the card facing the recipient. By doing so, the person will be able to read your card without having to turn it around.

When you receive another person's card, you should study it for a few minutes and comment on it before putting it in your card case. Do not casually put the card in your pocket, because it is considered an honor to receive a person's business card and it must be shown the proper respect.

Understand that if you have presented your business card to someone and they have not offered one in return, it may be because the person is not interested in developing a working relationship with you.

Business Entertaining/Dining

It is best to accept all invitations extended to you by Taiwanese business associates. However, if you must decline, be sure to give a good reason so that you do not cause the invitee to lose face.

Business meals will often include as many as 10 courses during a sit-down lunch or dinner. These meals are important for building a strong business relationship.

Toasting is a crucial component of business entertaining and will be done several times throughout the meal. In fact, seating will be arranged to ensure that those of equal rank are seated across from one another. In this way, you can personally toast the appropriate individual (that is, your counterpart).

When you are hosting a meal, be sure to pick up the bill. Note that it is customary for your Taiwanese associate or customer to offer to pick it up and perhaps even banter with you about it. One way to avoid such a scene is to take care of the bill away from the table by giving the server your credit card in private.

When you are in Taiwan, don't plan on going to bed early. Nighttime entertainment can last until the wee hours of the morning. If you are not a night owl by nature, you will probably have to push yourself in this regard, because you may be considered antisocial if you call it a night before others.

Dining is a joyous and largely social experience in Taiwan. Even if you are hosting the meal, be sure to defer ordering to your Taiwanese guests. Besides demonstrating your respect for their knowledge, you will also be certain that the appropriate portions will be ordered.

The Taiwanese take great pride in their food, which is one of the reasons that you will find it to be of such high quality. Specialty dishes include squid, clams, and oysters, which are often cooked in a wok. Some of the more unusual dishes include turtle, tiger, jellyfish, and snake.

Taiwanese etiquette dictates that you wait for your host to invite you to serve yourself. It also is considered good manners to try everything and make positive comments about the food, even if you do not find it to your taste.

Be sure to leave something on your plate when you are finished eating. This will communicate that you were satisfied with the meal.

You will be sure to impress your Taiwanese dinner mates if you are proficient with chopsticks. When you are serving yourself from community dishes, be sure to use the larger chopsticks that are available for serving purposes, rather than the ones with which you are eating.

Conversation

The Taiwanese way of beginning a meeting is by making small talk, so it is important to become acquainted with what should or should not be discussed. Appropriate conversational topics include your trip to Taiwan, what you have enjoyed about the country thus far, the weather, and information about the country you represent.

Another good topic of conversation is family. A wholesome family life shows good character, which is a valued trait by the Taiwanese.

When you are paid a compliment during a conversation, your response should express that you are not worthy of such praise. Whatever you do, don't acknowledge a compliment with a mere "thank you." Be as humble as possible.

Don't be surprised if your Taiwanese business associates ask what Westerners consider to be personal questions, such as, "What is your salary?" or "How much did that cost?" These questions are considered acceptable and should be answered, even if indirectly.

Topics to avoid include political affairs and communism.

Gestures and Public Manners

Keep in mind that although the Taiwanese may have many Western ways of doing things, their attitudes are still very much Taiwanese. For that reason, be sure to think the "Taiwanese" way as much as possible when conducting yourself both in public situations and during private meetings.

The concept of "saving face" is crucially important. For that reason, you should never embarrass anyone in public by losing your temper or raising your voice. Also reserve any criticism of a person for a private meeting.

Taiwan is very business-oriented. You must therefore understand that while you are there, your personal life will take a back seat to your professional one. Because the Taiwanese work ethic is so strong, it will not be uncommon for you to engage in work days of 12-15 hours.

Don't be offended by the lack of personal contact or not being acknowledged by the Taiwanese when you are in public. It's very common for people not to smile at others or engage in conversation with people they are passing on the street.

One way the Taiwanese maintain harmony is by couching a negative answer in a positive one. For instance, a "we will see" may really mean "we are not interested." "We will think about it" may imply "we are not interested in proceeding."

There is a lot of communication beyond the spoken word in Taiwan. For that reason, your eye contact, facial expressions, vocal tone, and gestures play an important part in relaying your message. Here are some do's and don'ts:

- Keep eye contact to a minimum, especially with those people who are more senior than you.

- Maintain a calm composure rather than displaying your emotions. This is an important part of "maintaining face."

- While personal space is important to Westerners, it is even more important to the Taiwanese. For that reason, be sure to stay a minimum of two arm's lengths away from another person, and also avoid touching others.

Gift-giving Etiquette

Gift-giving plays a significant role in establishing both personal and professional relationships. Because the Taiwanese tend to give very generous presents, Western visitors should be prepared to match this gift-giving enthusiasm. You will be especially pleased that you arrived with gifts in hand when you are given a present during your first meeting.

The Taiwanese custom is to refuse a gift politely when it is first presented. This formality should be continued until the giver insists that the gift be accepted. When this ritual is completed, the gift should be received with both hands, palms facing upwards.

Gifts are typically not opened in front of the giver, even if encouragement is given to do so. The thought behind this is that the person giving the gift may be embarrassed if it is of lesser value or quality than the one he or she received. Thus, wait until you are alone before you open any presents.

Appropriate gifts include anything that has to do with baseball or quality items carrying your organization's logo (gold Cross pens, paperweights, etc.). Be sure to take a variety of gifts, so that you can have at least one for any occasion.

Do not offend your Taiwanese business partner by giving something that may be appropriate in Western culture but is entirely inappropriate in Taiwan. This includes clocks and watches, which symbolize death, and anything that resembles cutlery (scissors, knives, etc.), as these types of items are thought to signify the severing of ties. Also, be sure not to give towels or handkerchiefs as gifts, because they are a sign of grieving.

The preferred colors of wrapping paper are red, gold, pink, and yellow. Avoid using black or white gift wrap.

Be careful about the number of presents you give someone. The Taiwanese place great emphasis on numbers and their meanings. Names, dates, and even license plates are chosen based on numerology. Here are some of the more notable meanings:

- 4: *Si* sounds like the Chinese word for "death." For that reason, doing things in fours or any reference to the number should be avoided.

- 6: *Lin* signifies the six Chinese elements of wind, river, lightning, mountain, sun, and moon. The term is thought to have a lucky meaning, so items in multiples of six may be given.

- 8: *Ba* sounds like "prosperity" in Chinese. Therefore, this number is a favorable one.

- 13: Just as in Western societies, this number is considered unlucky.

Red envelopes, also called *Hong Bao,* are given to every employee in Taiwan prior to the Chinese New Year, the Dragon Boat Festival, and the Moon Festival (see Holidays). These envelopes contain money. While bonuses may be given at other times throughout the year, the R.O.C. Labor Law requires that employees be rewarded in this way on these particular days. This is a government-mandated type of gift-giving that may be of importance to you if you are considered an "employer" in the country.

Greetings and Introductions

While bows are common in many Asian countries, this is not necessarily the case in Taiwan. The more common meeting ritual is a handshake, followed by the exchange of business cards.

You should acknowledge the most senior person first and give that person your full attention, followed by a handshake.

As in other Asian countries, there is a formality to exchanging business cards. Present your card with both hands and with the card facing the other person so that he or she can read it immediately without having to turn it around.

Arrangements should be made to have your business cards translated into Mandarin on the back. This can be done upon your arrival in Taiwan.

Note that when you are given the business card of a Taiwanese person, the first name you see will probably be the person's last name or family name, followed by the person's first name or given name. In addition, the Taiwanese may also have Western names for the benefit of the persons they will be meeting.

Always address the Taiwanese on a last-name basis (using "Mr.," "Mrs.," or "Miss"), unless you are asked to do otherwise.

Meeting Manners

Meetings usually begin with formal greetings, followed by a beverage (such as coffee or tea) and small talk before actually getting down to business. It is wise to allow your Taiwanese partner to initiate the business discussion.

Avoid discussing money early in a business relationship. While the Taiwanese recognize the importance of profit, this society encourages concern for the good of the whole and, thus, does not give precedence to money issues.

It is important for contracts to be in writing for Westerners, but in Taiwan, agreements are only as good as the piece of paper they are written on. Thus, Westerners should recognize that it is very common for negotiations to continue after an agreement has been signed.

The traditional way of signing or sealing a business deal is with a personal seal or "chops." This personal seal consists of an organization's symbol or logo etched in stone or wood, pressed in red ink, and placed on a document. If you foresee that a significant amount of business is going to be conducted in Taiwan, you should obtain a chop design for your organization.

Punctuality

Although the Taiwanese appreciate promptness, they do not view time with the same importance as the hurried Westerner. If you find you are going to be delayed for a meeting for more than 10 minutes, simply phone the people you will be meeting to advise them of your late arrival. Note: One way to avoid being late is to allow plenty of time when commuting by vehicle, because traffic jams are very common.

Seating Etiquette

The guest of honor should be seated facing the door with his or her back toward the wall. Hosts assume the seat opposite the person of his or her same level.

Seating is arranged in hierarchical order; therefore, it is best to wait to be told where to sit. The Taiwanese prefer to sit across from their business counterparts, rather than across from each other.

Tipping Tips

While tipping was not necessary at one time, it is now acceptable and is often expected. Restaurants and hotels automatically include a 10-percent service charge, but tipping is appropriate if unusual services have been requested or if the service surpasses normal expectations. The same recommended percentage applies to bellhops, chambermaids, or others who go beyond the call of duty for you.

If assistance is given taking your luggage from a hotel lobby to your room, be sure to display your appreciation by giving the porter approximately NT $80 per bag.

When traveling by taxi, be sure to give any change from your fare to the driver. In addition, if the driver assists you with your luggage, it is appropriate to tip him approximately NT $30 per bag.

When You Are Invited to a Taiwanese Home

It is most unusual to be invited to the home of a Taiwanese. So if you are, consider it quite a compliment. Be sure to take a small gift (other than food) and do arrive on time. You will be expected to remove your shoes and wear thong slippers that are given to you. Get ready to meet the entire family. If a meal is served, be sure to try everything and repeatedly comment on the excellent food.

Women in Business

Thanks to the international business scene, women are holding more responsible positions in Taiwan. However, there is still a well-defined line between the sexes and their professional roles in Taiwan and it may come as a surprise to a Taiwanese if one of the Western decision-makers is a woman. You should therefore forewarn and educate your potential Taiwanese business partners about any women who are key players on your team. This can be done through the correspondence you send prior to the meeting. Sharing this information will allow for no surprises and perhaps even assist a business deal in running more smoothly.

Whatever You Do...

- Don't invite your Taiwanese partner to breakfast. While business lunches and dinners are common, breakfast get-togethers are rare.

- Don't assume that just because you have a deal signed, sealed, and delivered, it means that business will be conducted based on the terms of the agreement. Many negotiations continue after a contract has been signed.

- Don't be too emotional when negotiating with the Taiwanese. You will do better if you mirror their body language and display less emotion in your facial expressions and tone of voice.

- Don't expect decisions to be made by a group of people. Taiwanese decisions tend to be made by individuals rather than by teams.

- Don't assume that deadlines will be met with the same promptness that they are by Westerners. Instead, think the Taiwanese way by anticipating that the deadline will be achieved seven to 10 days following the date it has been requested.

- Don't allow your first impression of Taiwan to be permanent. If you do not look beyond the traffic, pollution, and noise, you will miss the culture and beauty that lies beneath.

Advice From the Experts

"I have found that taxi drivers do not generally speak English. Have the hotel/host write your destination in Chinese so that you can show it to the driver. Also, have a hotel card in Chinese with you so that you can assure your return."

—*Douglas E. Darrow, International Operations Quality Leader, General Electric Aircraft Engine Services*

Chapter 12

Thailand

8 reasons people do business in Thailand

1. Corn, sugar cane, and tapioca are among Thailand's chief exports.

2. Manufacturing textiles is one of Thailand's strongest suits.

3. Thailand is also very strong in agricultural processing.

4. Thailand's chief crop is rice.

5. The country is a top producer of tin, tungsten, and gas.

6. Thailand is very strong in the tourism industry.

7. Thais are discrete people who keep criticism behind closed doors.

8. The people of Thailand not only have a strong work ethic, they also smile more than any other people in the world.

Thailand is located in the heart of Southeast Asia, between China and India, with Burma bordering it on the west and north, Laos on the northeast, Cambodia on the east, and Malaysia on the south. The country has distinct divisions of topography, with mountains in the north, dry plateau in the northeast, plains in the central part, and a tropical south on the coast, with beaches and numerous offshore islands. The population is close to 60 million people, the majority of whom are native Thais. Thailand's capitol is Bangkok, a beautiful city that includes a mixture of the old and the new, from primitive structures and traditions to pagodas, skyscrapers, and a bustling modern culture.

The name Thailand translates as "Land of the Free," an apt description. Thailand holds the distinction of being the only Southeast Asian country that has never been colonized. Once called Siam, its history dates back some 800 years, originating as an offshoot of the Khmer Empire, whose culture it adapted for its own. For many years, the people of Thailand enjoyed peaceful coexistence with its neighbors, until Burma invaded it in the 1700s and was later expelled by General Taksin and his followers. Upon Taksin's death, the current monarchical dynasty was established, starting with King Rama I. This line of kings included King Mongkut, Rama IV, who became famous in our century because of the popular stage and screen show, *The King and I*. Mongkut and his son, King Chulalongkorn, Rama V, paved the way for peaceable relations with the west by abolishing slavery and initiating numerous reforms in education, administration, and public welfare. Today Thailand is a thriving country whose daily life is strongly influenced by Buddhist teachings. It advertises itself as "The Land of Smiles."

Statistics and Information

Air Travel

When flying into Bangkok, you will land at the Don Muang Airport. There are several options for transportation into the city, including taxis, airport limousines, airport buses, and even a train to the station in Bangkok. Although the trip usually takes an hour from the airport to the heart of the city, it can take twice as long if the weather is bad.

Country Code

Thailand's country code is 66.

The major city codes are:

• 2 for Bangkok.

• 53 for Chiang Mai.

• 32 for Hua Hin.

• 38 for Pattaya.

• 76 for Phuket.

Currency

Thai currency is the *baht*. 25 *baht* is equivalent to US$1. Currency is available in one and five *baht* coins. Notes are available in 10 *bahts* (brown), 20 *bahts* (green), 50 *bahts* (blue), 100 *bahts* (red), and 500 *bahts* (purple). 100 *satang* is equivalent to one *baht*.

While banks give favorable currency exchange rates, authorized money-changers and hotels will also provide good rates, sometimes only slightly lower than banks. If you choose to exchange your currency at a bank, remember that they close by 3:30 p.m.

When exchanging traveler's checks for this country's currency, be sure to have your passport—you will need it for identification.

Dates

Dates are written in non-Western style as day, month, year. For example, January 30, 1999, would be written 30/1/99.

Ethnic Makeup

About three quarters of the population are native Thai. Individuals of Chinese descent make up 14 percent, and a mixture of minorities make up the remaining 11 percent, including Burmese, Indian, Khmer, Lao, Malay, and Mon.

Holidays

The following are the holidays that are celebrated throughout the country. It is wise to avoid scheduling meetings during these times.

January 1	New Year's Day
January/ February	Chinese New Year (the date varies, depending on the lunar calendar)
February/ March	Makhabucha Day (Buddhist New Year; the date varies, depending on the lunar calendar)
April 6	Chakri Day (a celebration of the founding of the royal dynasty)
Mid-April	Songkhran Day (Thai New Year)
May 1	Labor Day
May 5	Coronation Day
May 11	Harvest Festival Day
May 27	Buddhist Lent
May/June	Visakhabucha Day (a celebration of the birth, enlightenment, and death of the Buddha; this is the holiest of the Buddhist holidays; the date varies, depending on the lunar calendar)

July/August	Asalahabuja Day (a celebration honoring the beginning of the three-month Pongrains Retreat; the date varies, depending on the lunar calendar)
August 12	Queen's Day
October 23	Chulalongkorn Day (a celebration of the monarch from 1868 to 1919 who got rid of slavery)
December 5	King's Birthday
December 10	Constitution Day
December 25	Christmas Day
December 31	New Year's Eve

Language

Thai is the country's official language. English is the second-most spoken language.

Religion

Almost 95 percent of the population practices Buddhism, making Thailand one of the most strongly Buddhist countries in the world. Monks are revered, and throughout the country, the temple (wat) is the center of all communities.

Time Zone Differences

Thailand is:

- Seven hours ahead of Greenwich Mean Time.
- 12 hours ahead of U.S. Eastern Standard Time.
- Three hours behind Australian Eastern Time.

Weather

The climate in Thailand is hot and humid throughout the year. Temperatures can range from 68 to 91 degrees Fahrenheit. It can also be very rainy; downpours are common during May through September.

Etiquette

Business Attire

When packing for your trip, keep in mind that Thailand has a very hot and humid climate. Lightweight clothing in natural fibers will work best, depending on the time of year.

For outdoor activities and very cold air-conditioned environments, it is advisable to take along blazers, sweaters, and suit jackets.

Women will be most comfortable in lightweight dresses or skirts and blouses (with sleeves) for almost all occasions. Note that it is acceptable for women not to wear hosiery because of the heat. However, makeup should be worn.

The color black should be avoided, because it is the color associated with death.

Men will do well with trousers, white shirts, and ties for business situations. Some restaurants require jackets, so a sport coat or suit jacket is also recommended.

Recognize that the better dressed you are, the higher status you give yourself.

Business Entertaining/Dining

If you are invited to lunch, expect it to last two hours (that is, from 1 to 3 p.m.). This meal is typically for establishing rapport and developing relationships, which may take time.

Similarly, when you are invited to dinner, prepare to dine for a few hours (7 to 10 p.m., for example). Thai businesspeople want to know that they are compatible with you personally before developing a business relationship. The way you interact with them and the *sanuk* (fun) you have together during both business and social situations will be a determining factor in doing business with you.

Just as in many other parts of the world, whoever extends the invitation for the meal picks up the check.

When going to a restaurant, take your own alcohol. Sometimes even taking food is acceptable. Thais tend to eat dinner early, just as many *farangs* (foreigners) do (6 p.m. or so). If you plan on going to a Thai-owned restaurant, check the time it closes, because it is common for some of them to close earlier than you might expect (8 or 9 p.m., for example).

Be ready to *eat* when you visit Thailand! Believe it or not, Thai meals can consist of eight to nine courses—and spicy ones at that. In most restaurants, you will be seated at a revolving tabletop, allowing you to sample many tasty dishes.

Each person will be served a plate of rice. The community plates will include fish, pork, vegetable, and meat dishes. It is appropriate for someone to offer you a helping of one type of food at a time. In turn, you should reciprocate the favor for the person by placing food from one dish onto his or her plate over rice.

Thai manners dictate that you begin eating as soon as you are served, although it is appropriate for guests to wait for the host or hostess to take the first bite.

Most food is served to you in small pieces, so you will not be served a knife, only a fork and spoon. The fork, which should remain in your left hand, acts as a scooper for the food going into the spoon, which should remain in your right hand. If you have to cut something, it is appropriate to use the side of your spoon rather than the side of your fork to do so.

In areas of Thailand other than Bangkok, it is common for only a spoon to be used. Any additional assistance may come from the fingers of your right hand.

While in some Asian countries it is appropriate to wait for someone to serve you, if you are ready for more in Thailand, you may help yourself rather than wait to be offered the food.

In many other countries, serving utensils are offered, but this may not be the case in some Thai restaurants or even in some homes. It is often considered acceptable for a person to serve him- or herself using a used or unused spoon.

When eating, it is considered appropriate to eat a spoonful of rice and then another food, rather than first eating all the rice followed by all of something else.

If you are eating rice that sticks together, you may pick up the rice with your hands, form a ball, and eat it.

Note that the only time you will use chopsticks in Thailand is when you are eating noodles.

To drink soup or broth, do not lift the bowl and slurp it. Rather, use your spoon to sip it.

While individuals from some Asian countries eat in silence, it is appropriate in Thailand to make small talk while eating.

It is considered an honor to be offered the last helping in a serving dish. The proper etiquette is to wait until you are offered the serving and then tactfully decline the first time. If it is offered to you a second time and you want it, you may then accept it.

The last course that will be served to you is fried rice. As a way of displaying that you are content, it is better to leave it untouched.

Conversation

Politics and the royal family are great topics for conversation, just as long as they are discussed in a positive way. Additional conversational topics might include Thai places of interest and restaurants.

Don't feel people are being too inquisitive by asking such personal questions as, "How old are you?" The reason they ask such questions is to determine the level of respect you should be shown.

Although many people associate Thailand with *The King and I*, this is not a topic to be discussed with the Thais. Neither the play nor the movie has been shown in Thailand, probably because Thais consider it to be a lack of respect for one of their revered monarchs.

Although art and music are great topics of conversation in many countries, it is best to stay away from these subjects when making small talk with a Thai. This is because the Thai with whom you are speaking may not be familiar with those subjects and could be embarrassed by his or her lack of knowledge.

Gestures and Public Manners

You'll definitely want to be ready for the overwhelming smiles that you will receive from the Thais. After all, this is "The Land of Smiles." Thais smile for a variety of reasons, some of them obvious, others not so obvious. Because outward criticism is taboo, a Thai may even smile to indicate "I pardon you" or to excuse themselves when embarrassed.

A very important word to know is the bathroom, or the *hong Na-hum*. (Note: the literal translation is the "water room.") Men should ask for the *sukha-chai*, while women should ask the *sukha-ying*. When you finally find the room, be prepared to squat rather than sit. When you are finished, protocol dictates that you pour water from the available jug and then refill the water jug for the next person. Be sure to take plenty of tissue with you, because toilet paper is not common.

When walking into a room where a Buddha image is found, be sure to step over the threshold rather than walking on it. This is because, as in some other Asian countries, it is believed that souls live there.

Bus etiquette: Always remember that the back seat of a bus is reserved for monks.

When in a public location, such as a theater or auditorium, keep in mind that the front row is reserved for monks and high-ranking officials. Individuals of lesser status should sit behind them based on the rank and file order of the people who are present.

The Monarchy must be respected at all costs. Thus, keep your Thai banknotes in respectable places (never in your shoes or socks). In addition, always stand as a sign of respect when the Thai national anthem is being played.

Note that the appropriate way to sit is to kneel with your legs tucked under your body as you face the person of honor.

Your hands should always be clearly seen. This means keeping them out of your pockets and above a table. Your feet should remain close to your body rather than pointing outwards. Also note that it is rude to cross your legs whether you are sitting in a chair or on the ground.

Pointing is considered to be a faux pas in Thailand, so don't. In addition, never beckon to someone who is your equal or higher. When trying to get the attention of someone who is a subordinate, such as a server, do so by waving your hand with palm and fingers toward you.

Many Thais sit on the ground. Do not walk over them, but wait for them to make space for you to walk between them. As you pass, be sure to bend your body respectfully.

Gift-giving Manners

While in some Asian countries it is considered appropriate to exchange gifts at the first meeting, this is not the case in Thailand. Generally, gifts will be exchanged at a subsequent meeting. Be sure to bring a few gifts with you so that you are prepared. Your gifts may be quality brand name pens, pictures, or something that may be made in your home city.

When receiving a gift, thank the person for it and then set it aside. Do not open it in front of the giver, but wait until you are alone.

If you are invited to a Thai home, note that it is not absolutely necessary to take a gift. However, it is common practice to go with a small token or with flowers. Tulips and roses are appreciated, but marigolds and carnations are equated with funerals.

Unlike in other Asian countries, where it may be construed as a romantic gesture, perfume makes an excellent and much-appreciated gift for a Thai hostess. Your Thai host may appreciate a tie or a bottle of good liquor.

Presentation counts a great deal. A beautifully wrapped gift will leave a very favorable impression.

Thais consider odd numbers to be lucky, while even numbers are unlucky. This is something to remember should you give multiple gifts.

Greetings and Introductions

So many ways to wai: While handshakes are common among equals, the Thai greeting and acknowledgment, known as the *wai*, is a very important and varied form of communication for the Thais. The way to *wai* is to press your palms together with fingers pointing upwards, and lower your forehead to your thumbs.

Wai *to show respect:* Your *wai* is not only a greeting, it is also a sign of respect to others to be used when entering or passing sacred places. The presentation of your *wai* will vary, based on the person to whom you are extending it. If you are unsure of that person's status, keep your hands close to your body, with your forehead lowered to your thumbs and the tips of your fingers pointing straight down so that they are at neck level.

When meeting someone who is a subordinate, keep your fingertips held up, your thumbs closed and your forehead touching your thumbs, then bow so that your fingers are at chest level, as if you are meeting an equal or someone whose status you don't know.

When you are meeting someone who is a superior, your *wai* should be given by lowering your head to the point that your fingertips are above your nose.

In other situations, there's an even lower *wai*, which involves bending your body while lowering your forehead to your thumbs.

How to wai *when meeting a Buddha or a monk:* In this situation, it is appropriate to get on your knees to *wai*. Men do this legs bent under them, while women may sit with legs at one side. In this position, you should bend your body until your head barely touches the floor while facing the Buddha or monk being acknowledged. Rather than having your hands together as when you are standing, you should rest your palms on the floor. The ritual of bending to the floor and sitting up should be repeated three times (a lucky number in Thailand).

Know when to wai: For individuals from abroad visiting Thailand, rather than initiating a *wai*, it may be more appropriate only to respond to one. One reason is that the *wai* may not be appropriate for the circumstances and you may actually offend someone. For instance, never *wai* at someone who is providing a service for you (such as a waiter).

Proper forms of address: When addressing a Thai, it is appropriate to address this person by his or her first name preceded by the title "Mr.," "Mrs.," or "Ms." (for example, "Mr. Tom," "Mrs. Janet," "Ms. Mary"). One reason for this is that last names were not even used in Thailand until the beginning of the 20th century (about 75 years ago), so first names are more commonly used out of tradition and habit. Note that if a person has a title based on his or her profession, you should use it in the same way you would "Mr.," "Mrs.," or "Ms." ("Doctor Tom").

Handshakes: When meeting a man for the first time, a handshake is appropriate. However, when meeting a woman for the first time, substitute a smile for a handshake. Allow a Thai woman to initiate a handshake.

Responding to a Thai greeting: Rather than acknowledging another person with a "Good morning. How are you?," smiling or nodding is an appropriate greeting for people you see on a daily basis. Similarly, if a Thai asks, "Where are you going?" you are not being asked your itinerary for the day. Instead, the person is simply greeting you with the *farang* or Western equivalent of the greeting, "How are you?"

Meeting Manners

You will have a much better chance of meeting with high-ranking officials if you schedule your meetings prior to arriving in Thailand.

The reason you have requested a meeting should be made clear early in the appointment. Provide presentation literature that has been translated into Thai, as well as letters from other companies that have worked with you in the past or are currently working with you.

Keep in mind that the Thais are a bit less formal than others when conducting business. However, obvious breeches of Thai etiquette will be considered rude and will hurt your efforts.

Asking if there are any questions or opinions from your Thai associates should be done in an indirect manner. Blunt questioning is considered bad form.

The Thai team will want to meet several times with you and your team, as well as with you alone, before making any final decisions.

Punctuality

A lot of miscommunication has been caused because Thai time is divided into four- to six-hour segments, rather than 12-hour time frames. For instance, if you asked to arrange a meeting at 10 a.m., your Thai contact will interpret it as a 4 a.m. meeting. Of course, many Thais are accustomed to interacting with individuals outside Thailand who are on a 12-hour clock. However, it may be better to clarify times, rather than risk having people show up at two different times.

Although Thais believe in punctuality, heavy traffic can cause them to be late for meetings, so be prepared for this possibility.

Seating Etiquette

In Thailand, expect the man hosting the meal to sit next to his male guest. Similarly, the hostess will sit next to her female guest.

Tipping Tips

Tipping is common only in tourist areas. Note that leaving just one *baht* in Thailand is like leaving a penny for a server in the United States. If you are going to tip, try to be generous.

While most restaurants build in a 10-percent service charge, it is acceptable to leave a few *bahts* extra for exceptional service.

When taking a taxi, 10 percent of the full fare is an acceptable tip. However, if you have negotiated a price in advance with the driver, a tip is unnecessary.

For skycaps at the Bangkok International Airport and hotel porters, a tip of 5 to 10 *bahts* (20 to 40 cents) per bag is appropriate.

When You Are Invited to a Thai Home

The majority of entertaining will be conducted in public settings, such as restaurants, but if you are invited to a Thai home, consider it an honor. Before entering the home, check to see if your Thai host is wearing shoes. If not, be sure to also remove yours. Just as you should when entering a temple, step over the threshold rather than stepping on it.

Although it is not necessary, both the gift you take and the way it is wrapped will be much appreciated. If you know that the family you are visiting has children, have small gifts ready for them.

Although praise is appropriate, be very conservative when complimenting or commenting on an object in the home you are visiting because your Thai host may feel obliged to give it to you.

Women in Business

Although doing business with men is more common in Thailand, a woman who looks the part and acts it will be taken more seriously. Therefore, dressing well and conservatively is important.

Women should realize that a Thai man may wait to initiate a handshake with her, therefore, she should extend her hand first.

Respect is important, especially for monks. Women should never touch a monk or hand him an object directly.

While it may be acceptable for a "Western" businesswoman to extend a dinner invitation to her male client's spouse, this is not the case in Thailand.

Whatever You Do...

- Don't enter a Buddhist temple wearing shoes or a hat.
- Don't respond to "Where are you going?" by giving your itinerary for the day. A proper response would be "Down the street."
- Don't motion for someone to come to you by waving your fingers. Instead, do it with palms half closed, moving them towards you.
- Don't put a banknote in your shoe.
- Don't raise your voice if you get upset. Maintaining harmony at all costs is an important part of the Thai culture.

- Don't touch a Buddha or monk. It is a sign of disrespect.
- Don't sit in the last row of a bus. These seats are reserved for monks.

Advice From the Experts

"When establishing a joint venture, our Thai partners first wanted to establish a relationship with us. This was done over many delicious meals and socializing evenings."

—*Douglas M. Case, Douglas M. Case Law Office Inc.*

"Although Thais appear to be shy and retiring, they are formidable businesspeople not to be underestimated."

—*A vice president of a national materials manufacturing organization*

Chapter 13

Vietnam

8 reasons people do business in Vietnam

1. Vietnam is a leading manufacturer of textiles.

2. It is also a top manufacturer of chemical fertilizers.

3. Food processing is a major part of Vietnam's economy.

4. Many Vietnamese wish to become involved in foreign technology.

5. Vietnam's mineral resources include phosphates, coal, manganese, bauxite, chromate, and oil.

6. Vietnam has an abundance of crops in rice, sugar, fruits, vegetables, cassava, and corn.

7. The Vietnamese government encourages foreign partnerships as a way of employing its people.

8. The Vietnamese believe in forming business relationships that will last for many decades.

The Socialist Republic of Vietnam is located on the eastern part of the Indochina peninsula. Shaped like a letter "S," the country is bordered by China on the north and Laos and Cambodia on the west. The eastern and southern seaboards are the East Sea and the Pacific Ocean. Three quarters of the land consists of forest-filled hills and mountains, and there are thousands of rivers and streams throughout the country. Vietnam also has an abundance of natural minerals, including silver, gold, tin, coal, and precious stones, as well as oil and gas deposits in its numerous offshore islands.

More than 70 million people live in Vietnam, a country that was once divided into two separate north and south regions. A powerful force in Asia during ancient times, the country was once ruled by dynastic monarchies, and it also went through a period in the 1400s when it was under Chinese dominion. In 1858, the French invaded and conquered Vietnam, although they encountered much resistance. It took 30 years to establish full control and to create Indochina, a country that was an amalgam of Vietnam, Cambodia, and Laos. The imposition of French social and cultural mores, as well as their exploitation of the land and resources, created a growing resistance from the Vietnamese. At the conclusion of World War II, they successfully achieved independence from the French, and the Democratic Republic of Vietnam was established in September of 1945. However, two years later, the French were once more in control. The struggle for independence was renewed until the French were beaten in 1954. By this time, though, the nation had become divided in two, and years of internal strife and war followed. The United States eventually became involved in an effort to protect the region from falling under communist control. After many years of prolonged and escalated involvement, a peace was negotiated and U.S. military forces gradually withdrew from Vietnam. With the full withdrawal of U.S. troops in 1975 and Ho Chi Minh's subsequent overthrow of Saigon, the country became unified once more and Hanoi was established as the capital of the Socialist Republic of Vietnam.

Statistics and Information

Air Travel

Vietnam has two major international airports. Noi Bai Airport serves international and domestic travelers flying into Hanoi. This airport is approximately 45 km from the city. A taxi trip will take about an hour and a half and ranges from $30 to $40. Give yourself about an hour to get through customs, and expect to pay a $6 departure tax when leaving to fly to another country.

Tan San Nhat International Airport lies approximately 8 km from Ho Chi Minh City. Taxi fare is approximately $15 from the airport to the city. Departure tax is $8.

When traveling from either airport to your destination, be sure to have a map in hand, along with your destination written in Vietnamese. A taxi or private car is the most efficient form of travel to and from the airport.

Country Code

Vietnam's country code is 84.

The major city codes are:

- 4 for Hanoi.
- 8 for Ho Chi Minh City.

Most telephone numbers consist of seven digits.

Currency

The country's currency is the *dong* (VND). The *dong* comes in denominations of 100, 200, 500, 1,000, 10,000, 20,000, and 50,000. One *dong* is equivalent to 100 *xu* (cents).

The U.S. dollar is widely accepted, and many businesses (namely hotels) refuse to accept the dong from individuals who are not from Vietnam. For that reason, be sure to carry U.S. currency with you.

The best exchange rate in larger cities may be obtained from independent money-changers. Otherwise, use a bank for changing your currency.

When exchanging traveler's checks for this country's currency, be sure to have your passport—you will need it for identification.

Dates

When writing dates, indicate the day followed by the month and then the year. For example, June 22, 1999, would be written 22/6/99.

Ethnic Makeup

Like many ethnic groups in this area of the world, the Vietnamese are descended from the ancient Chinese and Mongols. Nearly 90 percent of Vietnam's population is Viet (or *Kinh*). There are 53 other ethnic groups, of which the majority are Hoa, a Chinese ethnic group. Other groups include Thai, Khmer Tay, Dao, Muong, and H'Mong. Each ethnic group has its own language and cultural identity.

Holidays

The following are the holidays that are celebrated throughout the country. Because these are considered national holidays, it is wise to avoid scheduling meetings during these times.

January 1	New Year's Day
Late January or early February	Tet (Lunar New Year)
February 3	Anniversary of the founding of the Communist Party

April 30	Liberation Day
May 1	International Labor Day
May 19	Ho Chi Minh's Birthday
June (8th day of 4th lunar month)	Buddha's Birthday
September 22	National Day
December 25	Christmas

Language

Vietnamese is the official language. You will also hear a variety of Chinese dialects, along with Russian, English, and French throughout the country.

Religion

Officially, the Socialist Republic of Vietnam is atheist. However, despite the government's attempts to squelch religion, many Vietnamese have continued to practice their religion. While more than half the population follows the teachings of Buddha, many people also practice Taoism and Confucianism, as well as Islam and Cao Daism. Approximately one tenth of the population practices Catholicism.

Veneration is a belief held by almost all Vietnamese. This is the idea that the dead are close by and have much control over the direction that life for the living takes. Many homes have altars designed to worship ancestors and to ask for their guidance in achieving fortune.

Time Zone Differences

Vietnam is seven hours ahead of Greenwich Mean Time and 12 hours ahead of U.S. Eastern Standard Time.

Weather

Vietnam's tropical climate keeps the temperature fairly pleasant but humid year-round. Visitors to the north will see temperatures from 60 degrees Fahrenheit in the winter (November-April) to 85 degrees in the summer (May-October). Summer is also the rainy season. In the south, temperatures from 76 to 85 degrees are consistent throughout the year.

Etiquette

Business Attire

Keep your dress professional and conservative. Men should wear conservative, American-cut suits. Women will do best with tailored skirted suits and business dresses, rather than slacks. A neat appearance will assist you in gaining more respect and help you represent your company in the most professional manner.

Because of the high humidity and temperatures, it is best to choose clothes made of lightweight and natural fibers. Whatever you do, be sure to avoid showy clothing and jewelry. The Vietnamese dislike people who flaunt their money.

Business Entertaining/Dining

A very important part of developing solid business relationships is the time you spend with your Vietnamese associates in social situations. One way to establish this rapport is by extending an invitation to lunch or dinner, or by accepting such invitations. Remember that the person who initiates the invitation always pays.

Be sure to arrive on time and stay until the host is ready to leave.

Unless your Vietnamese host initiates it, it is best not to discuss business in this type of social situation. Meals should be viewed as a tool for developing relationships and trust, as well as for learning about the Vietnamese culture.

Several dishes will be placed on a lazy Susan for everyone to share. Always wait to be invited to serve yourself and then try a bit of everything. Proper use of chopsticks will impress your hosts and show that you are interested in learning the Vietnamese way of life.

You may be offered many foods that are considered foreign to the Western diner—for example, bat meat, stir-fried baby birds, dog, and snake, to name a few. Be brave and taste a bit of everything so that you do not insult either the chef or the host. Because of Vietnam's long coastline, seafood is also abundant and very fresh.

Conversation

The Vietnamese are very inquisitive people who love lively conversation, especially with international visitors who are willing to share experiences unfamiliar to the Vietnamese. Expect to be asked personal questions about your marital status, children, and even salary. Family is the center of Vietnamese life, so asking about your associate's family and sharing the details and photos of your family is an excellent way to establish rapport.

Because the government often maintains significant control over its citizens' daily lives, it is advisable not to discuss politics. One reason is that you never know who may be listening to your conversation and report it to government officials. Keep your discussions light and broad.

Gestures and Public Manners

As a rule, most Westerners are taller than the Vietnamese and should take extra caution to maintain at least an arm's length distance, because the height may be perceived as threatening. If you find yourself facing another person on the bus or in a line, avoid making any physical or eye contact. Also refrain from making conversation.

When you are given a compliment, never accept it with a polite "thank you," as this is not compatible with the Vietnamese value of humility. Instead, make a point of disagreeing with the person who has bestowed the compliment.

The Vietnamese are serene, low-profile people who respect the same calm, controlled demeanor in people who visit and do business with them. Anything you do to call attention to yourself will be perceived as a lack of self-control, and may make the Vietnamese around you uncomfortable. Two ways to keep from drawing attention to yourself are to maintain a low pitch to your voice and to keep your gestures low-key. Other behaviors to avoid include:

- Pointing to another person to get their attention. If you must "beckon" to someone at a distance, begin by making eye contact with them. Then motion with your entire hand, palm up, and place it on your chest.

- *Never* show the soles of your feet, even when wearing shoes. This may mean you need to modify the way you sit. If you cross your legs, be sure the foot of the leg that is crossed points to the ground.

- Always maintain good posture. Balance is a revered principle and shows dignity.

- Use both hands to pass things to another person.

- Do not stand with your hands on your hips. This suggests aggression.

- Folding your arms across your chest will be viewed as a sign of disbelief or rejection.

Gift-giving Etiquette

Unlike in many other Asian countries, gift-giving is not essential for successful business transactions. However, this gesture is looked upon favorably and is also a great way to establish rapport.

The gift you present should reflect the level of the position the person holds. The most expensive gift should go to the most senior member of the team and move downward accordingly. Be sure not to present gifts of equal value to persons on different hierarchy levels.

Appropriate gift choices may include local crafts made of wood or stone, items with your company's logo, or books featuring your home region. Because of the huge tax imposed on alcohol, presenting a bottle of imported liquor will bring an enthusiastic response.

When choosing a gift, keep in mind that symbols such as the turtle, crane, and buffalo have positive meanings, while the monkey, cow, and pig are negative and should be avoided.

Red is the favored color of wrapping paper. Avoid wrapping a gift in white or black, because these colors represent death and sorrow, respectively.

As in most Asian countries, gifts should not be opened in front of the giver, but in private at a later time.

Greetings and Introductions

Formality is expected during business proceedings, especially in the initial greeting and exchange of introductions. Begin by shaking hands while bowing your head slightly and lowering your eyes. A two-handed shake, placing your left hand on the wrist of the other person, is a nice way to express your sincere interest in this meeting. Note that a woman from abroad should be the one to initiate a handshake with a Vietnamese man.

The use of proper titles is important. First names should never be used until you are invited to do so. As in many Asian countries, Vietnamese names begin with the surname, followed by the middle name, then the first or given name. Always precede someone's last name with a courtesy title of "Mr.," "Madame," or "Miss." (Note that "Madame" is used in place or "Mrs.")

Even after you have been invited to call a Vietnamese by his or her first name, it is still advisable to place a courtesy title in front of it. Here are some common terms of endearment:

- *ong*: older male

- *anh*: younger male

- *chi:* older female

- *co*: younger female

Although exchanging business cards is a less-formal affair than in other Asian countries, the Vietnamese are just as enthusiastic as other Asians about conducting such an exchange. Be sure to take a large supply with you and present your card just after the initial handshake.

It is a wise idea to have one side of your card translated into Vietnamese. If you are unable to have it done prior to your visit, this service can be arranged through your hotel concierge or business service center once you have reached Vietnam.

Meeting Manners

Business meetings with the Vietnamese are relaxed, lengthy affairs. Be sure to schedule ample time. Also, prepare to be invited to a meal following your meeting.

It is wise to arrange for a translator to be present to keep the proceedings running smoothly and to be sure you understand exactly what the Vietnamese are telling you.

The most senior member of the Vietnamese team will enter the room last and sit at the head of the table. However, don't be surprised if this person doesn't run the meeting himself and has appointed a junior member to lead the discussion.

A social exchange and the offering of tea or coffee may begin each meeting and last until the most senior Vietnamese member moves the discussion to business. Be patient. Attempts to rush the process will jeopardize your chances for a successful negotiation.

Having your business literature translated into Vietnamese will be appreciated and will move the meeting along more swiftly. Make a point of being direct when explaining your proposal and never be aggressive or demanding. Remember, humility is the key.

At the meeting's conclusion, allow time for the Vietnamese to ask questions and clarify points. Don't assume a smile is a sign of agreement or understanding. As in other Asian countries, a smile may mean anything from approval to irritation to confusion. If you are unsure of the situation, reiterate your points and ask if you have made everything clear.

Note that smoking is common and also acceptable in business meetings. It is not unusual for conference rooms to be full of smoke, something you have to endure if you do not smoke yourself. It is all right to decline a cigarette or cigar.

Because no single person is keen on taking the blame for when a decision goes bad, decision-making in Vietnam is often done by a group. This process can be slow and aggravating to the hurried Westerner, but showing these feelings will cause a rift in the relationship and may cause the deal to be called off completely. Thus, patience is important when waiting for a decision. Remember that the Vietnamese equate knowledge with power, and they will want to know all they can about you, your company, and the proposed deal before making any decisions.

The Vietnamese are astute in their business dealings. They know how to drive a tough bargain and are used to negotiating, because it is the norm for purchasing anything in Vietnam. While it is important to remain patient and reserved, don't take the Vietnamese for fools or you may be the one left holding the bag.

If you feel you have allotted ample time for a decision to have been made, one tactic sure to get a response is to mention that you are thinking of taking your business to another firm, city, or country. The Vietnamese are highly competitive people and knowing they may lose the deal will speed the process along.

Be careful with contracts. There are few to no restrictions governing contracts and commercial law in Vietnam.

Punctuality

Time in Vietnam is viewed in a less-regimented way than in the West. While your Vietnamese associates will try to be on time for appointments according to the flow of traffic, they may not necessarily get down to business and conclude meetings in a routine-like manner.

Any attempts to speed through your agenda will be considered rude and may even damage your chances for successful negotiations. Allow plenty of time for small talk. Business is conducted late into the evening in Vietnam and often includes a meal, drinks at a local disco, or perhaps even a visit to a karaoke club.

Seating Etiquette

There are no strict rules governing seating in Vietnam. However, it is a good idea to let your host show you where to sit.

Don't sit down until the senior-most member of the Vietnamese team has taken a seat.

Taxi Etiquette

Taxis are easily found in main attraction districts and in front of the classier hotels. However, finding taxis outside the main strip of a city is difficult.

Although taxi fares have fallen because of the growing number of taxi companies, drivers may still try to charge an exorbitant price. It is acceptable to bargain with a driver for a lower fee.

Tipping Tips

Service charges are added at many hotels and restaurants, so additional money is not necessary. The country doesn't officially allow tipping.

When You Are Invited to a Vietnamese Home

Because of the stronghold the government retains over business with individuals from abroad, many Vietnamese fear an invitation to their home will warrant government suspicion. Therefore, such invitations are very rare and should be accepted when extended.

When you are invited to a home, be sure to take a gift that will benefit the entire family. Separate gifts for the adults and children will be appreciated. Arrive punctually, but never early, because your hostess may still be cooking and may be unprepared for your early arrival.

You will probably be asked to remove your shoes and to wear house slippers provided by your host. Plan for a leisurely evening full of light conversation and hearty food.

Women in Business

Even though Vietnamese women are granted all rights under law, the reality is that there are few women in business in Vietnam, and men may feel awkward dealing with executive women. A Western woman can ease the situation by placing her name on top of all correspondence and emphasizing her accomplishments.

It is uncommon for women to travel alone in Vietnam, so taking along a companion or junior officer is advisable.

Whatever You Do...

- Don't let the soles of your feet show. This is considered a distasteful gesture, so be sure that your feet face the ground.

- Don't raise your voice or use highly animated gestures. These actions do not coincide with the Vietnamese principal of harmony, and may make those around you uncomfortable.

- Don't drink alcohol at business meetings if you are a woman. This behavior is associated with prostitutes and will hurt your chances of being taken seriously.

- Don't discuss politics or criticize the government in public or with people you hardly know. The Vietnamese government maintains a stronghold over its people and leaks to officials are common.

- Don't be alarmed if your Vietnamese associate takes your hand as you walk in public. This sort of public display by members of the same sex is an acceptable way of showing trust and a high level of comfort.

- Don't maintain long periods of eye contact with a Vietnamese. Prolonged eye contact is offensive and goes against the policy of avoiding confrontation.

- Don't forget to have your business cards and business literature translated into Vietnamese before arriving or soon after your arrival. Not only will doing so impress your associates, it will assist you in developing a solid business relationship.

Conclusion

You have now read that it takes a lot more to successfully conduct business outside your own country than merely greeting contacts and exchanging business cards. You have probably also learned that there is a unique art to doing business in Asia and the Pacific Rim. I hope that you will make this book one of your travel companions when visiting this part of the world.

Do you have a question about Asian or Pacific Rim business etiquette that was not addressed in this book? You can e-mail me at ateaseasia@etiq.com. Or contact me by writing to At Ease Inc., 119 East Court Street, Cincinnati, Ohio 45202, or by calling 800-873-9909. I can assure you of a prompt response.

Asian & Pacific Rim Etiquette HOTLINE

WHAT ETIQUETTE QUESTIONS DO YOU HAVE ON....
Appropriate Dress • Forms of Address • Business Card Etiquette
Topics To Avoid • Do's And Taboos • Seating Etiquette
Gift-Giving Manners • Business Entertaining • Tipping Tips

**E-Mail Your Questions To: ateaseasia@etiq.com
or Call Our Hotline at (800) 873-9909
Visit Our Website at http://www2.eos.net/atease/asia
119 East Court Street • Cincinnati, Ohio 45202**

Bibliography

Axtell, Roger. *Do's and Taboos of Hosting International Visitors.* John Wiley & Sons, Inc., 1990.

Bates, Chris and Ling-li. *Culture Shock: Taiwan.* Graphic Arts Center Publishing Company, 1995.

Bone, Robert W. *Maverick Guide To Australia.* Pelican Publishing Company, 1996.

Bone, Robert W. *Maverick Guide To New Zealand.* Pelican Publishing Company, 1996.

Bosrock, Mary Murray. *Put Your Best Foot Forward—Asia.* International Education Systems, 1994.

Braganti, Nancy and Devine, Elizabeth. *The Travelers' Guide to Middle Eastern and North African Customs and Manners.* St. Martin's Press, 1991.

Bullis, Douglas. *Culture Shock: Succeed in Business, Sri Lanka.* Graphic Arts Center Publishing Company, 1997.

Burbank, Jon. *Culture Shock: Nepal.* Graphic Arts Center Publishing Company, 1992.

Catley, Christine Cole. *The Xenophobe's Guide to The Kiwis.* Ravette Publishing, 1996.

Chambers, Kevin. *Culture Shock: Succeed in Business, Vietnam.* Graphic Arts Center Publishing Company, 1997.

Chesanow, Neil. *The World Class Executive.* Rawson Associates, 1985.

Cohen, David. *How to Succeed on Business Trips.* Sheldon Business Books, 1996.

Cole, Gregory. *Passport Indonesia.* World Trade Press, 1997.

Cooper, Robert and Nanthapa. *Culture Shock: Thailand.* Graphic Arts Center Publishing Company, 1996.

Craig, JoAnn Meriwether. *Culture Shock: Singapore*. Graphic Arts Center Publishing Company, 1993.

Curry, Jeffrey. *Passport Taiwan*. World Trade Press, 1998.

Curry, Jeffrey. *Passport Vietnam*. World Trade Press, 1997.

Draine, Cathie and Hall, Barbara. *Culture Shock: Indonesia*. Graphic Arts Center Publishing Company, 1996.

Dunung, Sanjyot P. *Doing Business In Asia*. Lexington Books, 1995.

Engel, Dean and Murakami, Ken. *Passport Japan*. World Trade Press, 1996.

Francia, Luis. *Passport Philippines*. World Trade Press, 1997.

Grzeskowiak, Andrew. *Passport Hong Kong*. World Trade Press, 1996.

Hoare, James and Pares, Susan. *The Simple Guide to Customs and Etiquette in Korea*. Global Books LTD, 1996.

Hunt, Ken. *The Xenophobe's Guide to The Aussies*. Ravette Publishing, 1993.

Hur, Sonja Vegdahl and Seunghwa, Ben. *Culture Shock: Korea*. Graphic Arts Center, 1993.

Kenna, Peggy and Lacy, Sondra. *Business China*. Passport Books, NTC Publishing, 1994.

Kenna, Peggy and Lacy, Sondra. *Business Japan*. Passport Books, NTC Publishing, 1994.

Kenna, Peggy and Lacy, Sondra. *Business Taiwan*. Passport Books, NTC Publishing, 1994.

Kingsland, Venika. *The Simple Guide to Customs and Etiquette in India*. Global Books LTD, 1996.

Kolanad, Gitanjali. *Culture Shock: India*. Graphic Arts Center, 1994.

Mansfield, Stephen. *Culture Shock: Laos*. Graphic Arts Center Publishing Company, 1997.

Morrison, Terri with Wayne A. Conway and George A. Borden, Ph.D. *Kiss, Bow, or Shake Hands.* Adams Media Corporation, 1994.

Munan, Heidi. *Culture Shock: Malaysia.* Graphic Arts Center Publishing Company, 1991.

Murray, Geoffrey. *The Simple Guide to Customs and Etiquette in Vietnam.* Global Books LTD, 1996.

Pascoe, Robin. *Culture Shock: A Wife's Guide.* Graphic Arts Center Publishing Company, 1992.

Perera, Audrey. *The Simple Guide to Customs and Etiquette in Singapore.* Global Books LTD, 1996.

Renwick, George W. *Australians and North Americans.* Intercultural Press, Inc., 1980.

Roces, Alfredo and Grace. *Culture Shock: Philippines.* Graphic Arts Center Publishing Company, 1994.

Seligman, Scott D. *Dealing With the Chinese.* Warner Books, 1989.

Sharp, Ilsa. *Culture Shock: Australia.* Graphic Arts Center Publishing Company, 1992.

Shelley, Rex. *Culture Shock: Japan.* Graphic Arts Center Publishing Company, 1995.

Sinclair, Kevin with Iris Wong Po-yee. *Culture Shock: China.* Graphic Arts Center Publishing Company, 1996.

Star, Nancy. *The International Guide to Tipping.* Berkley Books, 1988.

Tan, Raelene. *A Matter of Course: Chinese Etiquette.* Landmark Books, 1992.

Tan, Raelene. *A Matter of Course: Indian and Malay Etiquette.* Landmark Books, 1992.

Tonkin, Derek and Kongsiri, Visnu. *The Simple Guide to Customs and Etiquette in Thailand.* Global Books LTD, 1996.

Wei, Betty and Li, Elizabeth. *Culture Shock: Hong Kong.* Graphic Arts Center Publishing Company, 1995.

Wise, Naomi. *Passport Thailand.* World Trade Press, 1997.

Yang, J.C. *The Xenophobe's Guide to The Chinese.* Ravette Books, 1995.

Yip, George S. *Asian Advantage.* Addison Wesley, 1998.

About the Author

Ann Marie Sabath is the president of At Ease Inc., a 13-year-old Cincinnati-based company specializing in domestic and international business etiquette programs. She is also the author of *Business Etiquette in Brief* and *Business Etiquette: 101 Ways to Conduct Business With Charm and Savvy*, as well as executive editor of an Asian etiquette video series focusing on Japan, Hong Kong, Singapore, and Thailand.

Sabath's international and domestic etiquette concepts have been featured in *The Wall Street Journal, USA Today,* and Delta Airlines' *Sky Magazine.* They have also been recognized on *The Oprah Winfrey Show* and *20/20.*

Since 1987, Sabath and her staff have trained more than 30,000 people representing the business, industry, government, and educational sectors in how to gain the competitive edge. Her 10 Key Ways for Enhancing Your Global Savvy, Polish That Builds Profits, and Business Etiquette: The Key to Effective Client Services programs have been presented to individuals representing Deloitte & Touche LLP, Fidelity Investments, General Electric, Procter & Gamble, Arthur Andersen, MCI Telecommunications, The Marriott Corporation, and Salomon Brothers, among others.

In 1992, At Ease Inc. became an international firm by licensing its concept in Taiwan. In 1998, the firm also established its presence in Egypt and Australia.

Her forthcoming books, *International Business Etiquette: European Manners* and *International Business Etiquette: Latin and Central America,* will be released in 1999.

Index